Applied Change Management

Approaches to Organizational Change and Transformation

By Walter R. McCollum, PhD

Foreword by Raghu Korrapati, PhD

Afterword by Charles Edebiri, MS

Published by

McCollum Enterprises, LLC

Dr. Walter R. McCollum

www.mccollumenterprisesllc.com

info@mccollumenterprisesllc.com

(866) 512-6839

Fort Washington, Maryland

ISBN 978-0-9791406-1-7

All Rights Reserved, Copyright 2007

No part of this book may be reproduced or transmitted in any form or by any means, graphic, electronic, or mechanical, including photocopying, recording, taping, or by any information storage retrieval system, without the permission in writing from the publisher.

Dedication

To my grandfather, Walter D. McCollum, Sr., in loving memory. To my grandmother, Mary Louise McCollum.

This book is dedicated to Organizational Development and Transformation consultants, academicians, organizational leaders, students and researchers in their quest to impact organizational change.

"I can do all things through Christ which strengthens me." — Philippians 4:13

Acknowledgements

To my mother, Katherine B. Garner, and my father, Walter D. McCollum, Jr. Thanks for loving me unconditionally.

To my family members and friends. Thanks so much for the continued love and support.

To my Walden University students. Keep pursuing your educational endeavors and aspirations of becoming scholar practitioners.

To Pastor Marquis Townes, and the Salem Zion Baptist Church Family. Thanks for always supporting me.

To my pastors, Rev. Dr. Grainger Browning Jr. and Rev. Dr. JoAnn Browning. Thanks for being such phenomenal examples and global leaders.

To my mentors who saw potential in me. Thanks for your guidance, leadership, encouragement, and love. I am so grateful. Your example has helped me mentor others academically, professionally, and personally.

To my brother Robere' Brunson. Thanks for your fellowship and kindred spirit.

To Dr. Colleen Hawthorne. Thanks for your encouragement, support, guidance and genuine friendship.

To Dr. Marilyn Simon. Thanks for being the greatest humanitarian ever. Thanks for your mentorship and friendship.

To Dr. Raghu Korrapati. Thanks for your guidance and friendship. Also, thanks for writing the Foreword in this book.

To Charles Edebiri. Thanks for your brotherhood, friendship and fellowship. Also, thanks for writing the Afterword in this book.

Father God, in the name of Jesus, thank you for my life, health, and strength. You are worthy and have all power in your hands to do all righteous things. For you are God and God alone. There is none above you, beneath you, nor beside you. How Excellent is your name in all the Earth. Thank you for my family and friends and the support they continue to provide me. Thank you for your grace and mercy. Thank you for the favor you continue to place on my life. I am so grateful. Thank you for your darling Son Jesus, who died on the cross so that we may have abundant life. Thank you for Calvary. Thank you for the bright and morning star. Thank you for the fortitude to write this book. I pray that it will be received as a tool kit to help consultants, academicians and organizational change leaders globally in their quest to impact change. Thank you for allowing me to accomplish my educational endeavors. Thank you for such wonderful career opportunities. Thank you for my spiritual gifts, talents, and my light that shines so that others can see your good works. Thank you for defining and confirming my purpose in life and supplying me with the necessary tools to employ it. All of these blessings I pray in Jesus' name. Amen.

Table of Contents

Foreword – 11

Introduction – 13

Chapter 1: Business Ethics and Corporate Responsibility – 23

Chapter 2: Communication and Leadership – 31

Chapter 3: Marketing and Branding – 57

Chapter 4: Human Resources Strategy– 75

Chapter 5: Decision-making and Valuation – 93

Chapter 6: Program and Project Management – 121

Chapter 7: Organizational Change and Transformation – 141

Chapter 8: Finance and Investments – 185

Afterword – 249

Foreword

This book presents and compares several influential theories of organizational development and change management in practice today. Dr. McCollum, now Manager for Transformation Consulting at Capgemini, briefly outlines a number of practical, common sense, systematic approaches to managing change in organizations.

Dr. McCollum does an excellent job of delineating the major theories of organizational development with an emphasis on the strengths and weaknesses of these theories relative to change management and transformation. He articulates with clarity the manner in which the major theorists of this field evolved and interrelate with one another. He presents a comprehensive assessment of theories and their role in transforming the present day organizations in the applied management context.

Applied Change Management: Approaches to Organizational Change and Transformation locates change management strategies and practices within the broader context of becoming familiar with the unique organizational culture of one's own organization. The information presented in this book is particularly important for new managers who see opportunity for change everywhere but who must be cautious and courteous when implementing these changes. For new managers, and for those who need to refresh on their managerial skills, this book is an essential resource for understanding the social, political, economical, and technical challenges involved in change management and transformation.

Dr. McCollum defines change in general, and in an organizational setting before addressing the importance of change management skills in organizations and the ability of managers to recognize how they themselves react to change. The examples of actual management experiences provide practical advice within the context of cited research to help the reader identify problem-solving techniques including assessment models in an organizational and information environment. The Programme Management Maturity Model (PMMM) developed by ProgM, for instance, provides a mechanism through which an organization can assess itself. Finally, this book is useful to Organizational Development and Transformation consultants, academicians, organizational leaders, students, and researchers in their quest to influence organizational change.

Raghu Korrapati, Ph.D
Editor-in-Chief
International Journal of Applied Management and Technology
http://www.ijamt.org/

Introduction

"Perception is strong and sight weak. In strategy it is important to see distant things as if they were close and to take a distanced view of close things" - Miyamoto Musashi 1584-1645, legendary Japanese swordsman

For centuries people in this country have come together and performed tasks to achieve common goals. Initially these collaborative efforts were uncomplicated and consisted of only a few working together with a succinct understanding of the relationship between them. In other words, who was to perform which tasks was clearly defined as well as who was to be "in charge" was also.

The industrial revolution ushered in a change in that structure. Masses of individuals would merge in one location to perform selected repetitive tasks under the direct supervision of a few. The hierarchy was clear; there were few levels on the ladder – one level for workers, another for bosses and the top level for owners.

This mechanistic structure of organizations worked for many years until those on the bottom as well as those on the top of this ladder responded to the increasing pace of change going on around them. European and Asian countries were building, or in some cases rebuilding, themselves up to levels competitive with the United States. At the same time American workers' attitudes toward work began to change. Business owners wanted more and better production from workers, and workers wanted to share more equally in the wealth, created by their labor, as well as to increase the amount of comfort and leisure.

New ways had to be devised to mesh these two seemingly conflicting interests – one of greater production and the other of more humane treatment. To meet this challenge, social scientists from many disciplines including sociology, psychology, anthropology, and economics fashioned a structure consisting of many management tools, concepts and techniques, or what is more commonly called organizational development (OD) or organizational transformation. This creation was designed to deal with the changing times and attitudes that organizations had to contend with.

Organizational development (OD), a process derived from 1950's sensitivity training (Michael, et. al, 1981) and survey feedback (Burke, 1981), is often explained in a variety of ways. According to Michael et al. (1981) it is a technique of organizational change. W. Warner Burke defines it as "a process of applying knowledge from the behavioral sciences toward changes in an organization's culture so that individual needs and organizational goals can be integrated more effectively" (Burke, 1981, p. 190). According to Burke, OD is synonymous with change, but not necessarily the other way around. He proposes that there are three criteria to determine an OD – based intervention:

1) it responds to the needs of the organization's members for change;
2) the organization's members are involved in the planning and implementation of change; and
3) the organization's culture is changed.

The final criterion of Burke's explanation of organizational development is the most debated (Burke, 1981).

Bennis (1969) defines it as, "... a response to change, a complex educational strategy intended to change the beliefs, attitudes, values, and structure of organizations so that they can better adjust to new technologies, markets, and challenges, and the dizzying rate of change itself."

Beckhard (1969) defines it yet another way. According to him OD is "an effort (1) planned, (2) organization-wide, and (3) managed from the top, to (4) increase organization effectiveness, and health through (5) planned interventions in the organization's process using behavioral science knowledge" (Burke, 1981; Beckhard, 1969). Although all of these explanations of organizational development speak to aspects of change, it is Beckhard's definition that is the most widely accepted and used (Burke, 1981; Beckhard & Harris, 1977).

In spite of this widely accepted definition, though There are some experts who refute specific aspects of Beckhard's premise. Beer and Huse disagree with

Beckhard stating that organization development should be "managed from the top" and argue that it can begin anyplace in the organization. They also contend that top management should not be too committed to change, particularly in its initial stages, because it could lead to resistance by subordinates. They further argue that managing from the top means managing the process and not the content (the specific unit changes and what the organization should become). This action, they maintain, can lead to resistance to the desire of change. They contend that in order to nullify some of this resistance that those affected by the change should manage the content (Burke, 1981).

According to Burke (1981) the evolution of OD came about as an imperative for dealing with the bureaucratization of organizations. Beer (1980) sees it as being brought on by the "crisis in commitment and adaptability" along with the "development of applied behavioral science knowledge". He defines it as "a process for diagnosing organizational problems by looking for incongruencies between environment, structure, process and people (Beer, 1980)."

Regardless of which definition of organizational development one accepts it can be agreed that OD represents at the very least, an attempt at change. It also attempts to meet specific goals and is carried out in a particular process. The goals of OD typically include:

1) *better use of human resources;*

2) *the design, or redesign, of the communication process;*

3) *the development of reward systems that cater to the higher order needs of individuals;*

4) *involving people in the decision-making process; and*

5) *creating a more humane working environment*

Its process typically includes six steps:

1) entry (the point when an organization's leadership recognizes it needs help);

2) contractual agreement with a consultant;

3) data collection by the consultant about the organization from its members, documents and observations;

4) feedback from the consultant to the organization's leaders regarding the data analysis;

5) suggested intervention; and

6) an evaluation of the OD processs.

According to Beer (1980), organizations do not change until they are forced to do so. This force can be either internal or external. Internal pressures that typically lead to change are high levels of turnover, absenteeism, grievance rates, complaints and hostilities; and even sabotage and strikes. External pressures include the inability to remain competitive, consumer and community interests groups and government legislation. Beer (1980) also cites crisis as a motivator for change and indicates that it is important in the creation of a readiness state for change. He also warns that unless dissatisfaction and a desire for something new exists at the top level of management, no change in a hierarchical organization will occur (Beer, 1980).

Beer (1980) devised a formula for change similar to that created by Gleicher and used by Beckhard and Harris (1977). His change formula is as follows:

$$Ch = (D \times M \times P) > C$$

Change (Ch) only occurs when there is sufficient dissatisfaction (D) with the status quo, a new model (M) for managing has been defined and when the process for how change is to be managed is "well" planned (P). If these factors are greater than the costs (C), then the change effort will be initiated (Beer, 1980).

Deciding upon which approach to use is the greatest and most significant problem of organizational change (Beer, 1980). Regardless of which method is selected all organizational change efforts and techniques share common goals. These include better performance, increased motivation and cooperation, better communication; and reduced absenteeism, turnover, costs and conflict (Szilagyi & Wallace, 1983). Just as with organizational development, there is disagreement about how change should be implemented, and the very techniques utilized to generate organizational change have themselves undergone transformation.

Harold Leavitt (1965) describes four approaches to organizational change: structural, technological, task and people (actors). Structure refers to the communication, authority (or roles) and workflow systems. Arrangements of the workflow and physical layout are embedded in technological changes. Tasks are the specific jobs performed and include job design. Incorporated in the people factor are attitudes, motivation, training, selection, and performance appraisal (Szilagyi & Wallace, 1983; Lea vitt, 1965). Leavitt (1965) contends that changes in one system will influence the others.

Classical organizational theorists concentrated heavily on structural change. These deductive methods called for an analysis that reverted from tasks back to divisions of labor and authority systems. This often led to legalistic and ethical assumptions about human beings; one assumption being that people will carry out all the tasks required of their jobs simply because they have contracted to do so. They also fostered the assumption that people, if informed of the organization's goals, will put forth all of their efforts to achieve them. Structural approaches, therefore, emphasize order, discipline authority and hierarchy (Leavitt, 1965).

Outgrowths of the structural change approach include "decentralization" and the "engineering" approach. The belief behind decentralization is that by creating smaller, more autonomous units, motivation and goal -oriented behavior will increase.

The increase of autonomy within these units is considered to be an impetus for even further change. The engineering approach seeks to modify people's behaviors in order to enhance task performance through altering the organizational structure; hence, it is considered to be "social engineering" (Leavitt, 1965).

Because of the critical impact of the role of technology on organizations, it has effected organizational change. Taylor's Scientific Management of the 1930s and 1940s was the first to venture into this technique of organizational change. It was considered by many to be, as Leavitt (1965) states it, "ahuman", and, to some, inhuman because of its removal of the thinking process from the work and its reliance on physical labor. These methods did not address organizational problems that involved judgment or informational tasks (Leavitt, 1965).

In spite of the shortcomings of Taylorism, scientific management did not die out. Other technological approaches such as operations research, an invention of the World War II era, and information processing techniques, a contemporary of the computer age, came along. Like Scientific Management, both of these techniques usually separated the planning of problem solving from solution implementation; hence, the worker is left with less to think about. However, they differ from Scientific Management in that they are applicable to a greater variety of tasks (Leavitt, 1965).

The recent literature dealing with organizational change mostly comes from a people approach framework. These approaches attempt to effect change by first altering the behaviors of those who are expected to carry out the direction that will help the larger organization to meet its goals. Creators and practitioners of this approach argue that by changing human behavior, a change in other aspects of the organization, such as structure task performance, will occur (Leavitt, 1965).

These models have moved through two phases: manipulative and power -equalization. Social scientists such as Dale Carnegie and others delved into the work of how to overcome resistance to change. In doing so, however, they hit what Leavitt (1965) terms as a "soft spot", as many began to question the ethical and methodical underpinnings of these scientist suggested techniques. These approaches responded to the question: "How can we get people to do what we want them to do?" (Leavitt, 1965).

The creation of the power equalization approaches came out of client-centered therapy and group dynamics. The aim is to allocate equal power to those who are expected to change. Major emphasis are placed upon not only changing people first, but on affect, morale, sensitivity, and psychological security. Internally generated change in individuals, groups and organizations are most valued. Such beliefs have been fostered in the writings of Argyris; Lippitt, Watson and

Westley; Bennis, McGregor and Likert (Leavitt, 1965).

As organizations continue to merge with and acquire other organizations, it is imperative for organizational leaders to determine which organizational change and transformation approaches are best suited for the change. This book outlines and explains a myriad of proven methodologies and approaches to organizational change and transformation, that has been used by many organizations across various industries, to help achieve their organizational goals and objectives.

Chapter 1 - Business Ethics and Corporate Responsibility

"It is a commonplace executive observation that businesses exist to make money, and the observation is usually allowed to go unchallenged. It is, however, a very limited statement about the purposes of business" - Daniel Katz and Robert L. Kahn in the Social Psychology of Organizations (1966)

Clarkson Principles for Stakeholder Management

The Clarkson Principles were formulated at the Clarkson Center for Business Ethics in the early to mid -1990s, years before scandals shook the corporate world. Stakeholder theory was an emerging field of study at the time, and some conferences were held for management students to gather and share ideas on this new concept. The Clarkson Principles represent an early stage general awareness of corporate governance, the importance of which can now only be fully appreciated in hindsight. There are seven principles.

1) Managers should recognize and monitor the concerns of all stakeholders when making decisions

2) Managers should openly communicate with stakeholders about their respective concerns

3) Managers should be sensitive to the concerns of stakeholders

4) Managers should endeavor to distribute the burdens as well as the rewards among stakeholders

5) *Managers should work cooperatively with public and private sectors to minimize risk arising from corporate activities*

6) *Managers should avoid any risks or activity that might jeopardize human rights*

7) *Managers should recognize potential conflicts between their own role and the legal and moral responsibilities of the stakeholders. Each conflict should be handled by open communication and possible third party arbitration*

Soft Systems Methodology

Sometimes in business it is necessary to apply Systems Thinking to non-systematic situations. Formulated by Peter Checkland, it is a qualitative technique that is primarily used in situations that involve social, political and human activity. Checkland's research pointed out those using Hard Systems approaches, which are perfectly effective when dealing with technology issues, is inadequate for large, complex organizational issues. The reason is because they do not take the human factor into account. Soft Systems Methodology corrects this. The steps employed are as follows:

1) *Investigate the unstructured problem*
2) *Express the problem situation through "Rich Pictures. Which are a means of capturing information like boundaries, structure, information flows*

and communication channels

3) *Root definitions of relevant systems. From what different perspectives can this problem be approached. Root definitions are written as sentences that elaborate a transformation. It has six elements summed up as CATWOE, Customer, Actor, Transformation process, Waltenschaung (German for Free World View), Owner and Environmental constraints*

4) *Conceptual models, formal system and other system*

5) *Comparison of #4 with # 2*

6) *Feasible, desirable changes*

7) *Action to improve the problem situation*

The main benefit of SSM is that it applies a systemic approach to a non -systemic situation. It is specifically tailored toward the human factor that is always present in business, and readily acknowledges that people cannot be dealt with in the same manner as computers or other machinery.

Dialectic Inquiry

A theory of philosophy, which has evolved over the ages. It has a number of business applications. The Asian concept of opposites, Ying and Yang, is one branch of this philosophy. The Greek version is that all change comes through the struggle of opposites.

The theory died out in the West until the time of Kant and Hegel during the Industrial Revolution in the 20th century. It became a layered process of arriving at the truth by lacing contrary positions in juxtaposition to one another.

Another definition is that it is a philosophical term applied to methods of debate that seek to prove or disprove something by rules of reason. In general, what emerges as the most consistent aspect of this philosophy is that it is a thinking communication process based on changing things.

Conflict of Paradoxes.

In dealing with ethics, which is complex by nature and deals with contradicting forces, Dialectic Inquiry provides a very practical way to simplify arguments and provide clear and sharp contrast for opposing viewpoints.

Bottom of the Pyramid

Writer/economist C. K Prahalad wrote a book that starts out with this undeniable premise: Most of the population of the earth is poor. Four billion of the planet's six billion people live on less than $2.00 per day. For more than fifty years, the great institutions of the world and also rich countries and organizations have done their best to help, but have been unable to wipe out poverty.

Prahalad says that "if we stop thinking of the poor as victims or as a burden and start recognizing them as resilient and creative entrepreneurs and value conscious consumers, a whole new world of opportunity will open up." In other words, rather than viewing the world's poor as a problem that drags down the global economy, they should instead be considered as an asset with vast potential. To transform this theory in to realty, he suggests twelve principles of innovation:

1) Focus on quantum leaps in price performance

2) Hybrid solutions, blending old and new technology

3) Scaleable and transportable operations across countries culture and languages

4) Reduced resource intensity: eco-friendly products

5) Radical product re-design, marginal changes to existing Western products will l not work

6) Build logistical and manufacturing infrastructure

7) De-skill (service) work

8) Educate semi-literate customers in product usage

9) Product must work in hostile environments: noise, dust unsanitary condition, abuse, electric black-outs, water pollution

10) Adaptable user interface to heterogeneous consumer bases

11) Distribution methods should be designed to reach both highly dispersed rural markets and highly

dense urban markets

12) *Focus on broad architecture, enabling quick and easy incorporation of new features*

This theory challenges us to reconsider and change long held beliefs, assumptions and ideologies to eliminate poverty. The poor should not be viewed as victims, Prahalad argues, but rather as "resilient and creative entrepreneurs and value - conscious consumers." He maintains that "Bottom of the Pyramid" consumers are very much open towards advanced technology and therefore should be able to fully participate in the benefits of globalization. Prahalad even goes so far as to speculate that embracing this innovative way of thinking can lead to a new wave of global prosperity.

Stakeholder Value Perspective

Corporations influence our society so much that it is now recognized that they have obligations that reach beyond simply their own bottom line. Corporations also have certain social and moral responsibilities. Academics in such fields as law, political science and sociology examine corporate responsibility in great detail in order to determine what constitutes a responsible Corporation. One of the best methods is to study the topic from the perspective of stakeholders.

The Stakeholder Value Perspective recognizes that Corporations are networks of parties and people working together towards a shared goal. This includes the external players (customers, suppliers and government) as well as those directly employed by the company.

The Stakeholder Value Perspective emphasizes responsibility over profitability and sees organizations primarily as coalitions, which must serve all parties involved? And thus the success of such an organization should be measure by the satisfaction among all stakeholders, internal and external. Advocates of this view insist that all stakeholders share an equal moral claim on the organization. Such an understanding, they say, will benefit not only the company itself, but it will also contribute to the overall health of society.

Chapter 2 - Communication and Leadership

"Management is doing things right; leadership is doing the right things" - Peter F. Drucker, American Managem ent Guru

Consensus-seeking Tendency in Groups

Groupthink Theory, developed by Irving Janis, argues that group cohesiveness and solidarity are more important than considering the facts in a realistic manner. In their zeal for unanimity, members of such a group will often ignore or overlook certain facts in their decision -making processes that might lead to a conclusion different from the rest of the group. Groupthink typically has the following features:

1) The group is highly cohesive

2) The group is isolated from contrary opinions

3) The group is ruled by a directive leader, who makes his or her wishes known

Though maintaining harmony within a group obviously has benefits, it has consequences as well. For example, the members tend to not seek out professional opinions if they will be at variance with the group's conclusions. Furthermore, the group usually does not have any contingency plans, because they are over- confident in their decisions. Janis also points out that Groupthink has a coercive effect that limits free thinking and inhibits creativity.

Scenario Planning

If a company is going to plot a logical course of action for the future, it needs a model that can help it envision different outcomes. Scenario planning is a method for helping a company to do that in an organized, logical fashion.

It is a group process that requires cooperation and an active exchange of knowledge. What is being determined are different possible outcomes, or scenarios, based on different decisions the company could potentially make. Each possible scenario is considered a "story." In this way, it can easily be communicated to others who have a stake in the decision - making process. The following eight steps are essential to the scenario planning process:

1) *Identify people who will contribute a wide range of perspectives*

2) *Conduct comprehensive interviews/workshop s about how participants see big shifts coming in society, economics, politics, technology, etc*

3) *Group (cluster) these views into connected patterns*

4) *Group draws a list of priorities (the best ideas)*

5) *Create rough pictures of the future, based on these priorities, stories and rough scenarios*

6) *Add further details to impact scenarios. Determine in what way each scenario will affect the corporation*

7) Identify early warning signals and things that are indicative for a particular scenario to unfold

8) The scenarios are monitored, evaluated and reviewed

Experts that work with scenario planning caution against treating scenarios as an informational or instructional tool rather than for participative learning and/or strategy formation

Metaplan

This is a model for developing opinions, building understanding, and formulating recommendations and action plans to solve problems. An important part of this approach is to break up larger problems into their smaller constituent parts. People working on these problems can, in turn, be broken into smaller groups concentrating on specific objectives.

The technique was developed in Germany in the 70s by two brothers, Wolfgang and Eberhard Schnelle. It has the advantage of involving a large number of people in the task of problem-solving, and helps to save time by avoiding duplication of efforts and long, inconclusive decision - making processes.

The Metaplan approach does, however, have certain disadvantages, such as the costs of using specialized materials and the reluctance of some people who, though competent, are not eager to speak in public.

Using a Metaplan makes the most sense in situations when group involvement and a vigorous exchange of ideas are required. It can often be a useful way of structuring the creative process.

Strategy Maps

What does an organization do when it needs to understand the cause and effect relationships of strategic objectives in order to create value? One technique is to use strategy maps. These are diagrams that consider via the four Balanced Scorecard perspectives: financial, customer, processes, and learning and growth. It contains all of the relevant information on one page, using connecting arrows to describe cause and effect relationships.

Strategy maps are a very beneficial means of describing a strategy and communicating it to both executives and employees. This makes it easier to successfully implement the strategy.

Enterprise Architecture

This model has been popular since 1987, when it was first introduced by John Zachman. It provides a blueprint, or architecture, for the organization's current and future information infrastructure.

What is innovative about this approach is that it is centered on points of view, whereas previously the process had been considered as a series of steps. The following is the list of players in the Enterprise Architecture Framework:

1) Someone who has undertaken to do business in a particular industry
2) Business people who run the organization
3) Systems analyst who wants to represent the business in a disciplined form
4) Designer, who applies specific technologies to solve the problems of the business
5) Builder of the system
6) System itself

To properly understand Enterprise Architecture, it's imperative to be familiar with the proper definition of the term. An "Enterprise" is a business association consisting of a recognized set of interacting business functions. It is capable to operate as an independent, standalone entity. "Architecture" is defined as the set of principles, guidelines, policies, models, standards, and processes that aligned with business strategy and information requirements, that is guiding the selection, creation and implementation of solutions that are aligned with future business direction.

Identifying Sources of Power

This is a theory developed by French and Raven that identifies six bases of (sources of social organizational) power. The following are the different bases of power that they have defined:

1) Reward power: Based on the ability to give positive

consequences or remove negative ones

2) *Coercive power: This is the perceived ability to punish nonconformists*
3) *Legitimate power: Someone is authorized to direct and command*
4) *Referent power: Power achieved through association with others*
5) *Expert power: Based on having distinctive knowledge or expertise*
6) *Information power: Information needed by others in order to reach a goal*

This theory argues that the reaction of the receiving agent (not the person in power) is the more useful focus for explaining the phenomena of social influence and power. Attraction and/or resistance are the recipient's two potential sentiments towards the agent that uses power.

Leadership Continuum (Comparing Autocratic vs. Democratic Leaders)

According to the model of R Tannebaum and W. H. Schmidt (1973) an autocratic leader will likely make his own decisions. This would be an individual who tends not to delegate. In sharp contrast, the democratic leader gives subordinates more decision making ability.

The following forces are important for leaders to consider:

1) *Forces in the manager: belief in team member participation*
2) *Forces in the subrogate person: subordinates who are independent, tolerant of ambiguity, competent, identify with organizational goals*
3) *Forces in the situation*
4) *The team has requisite knowledge*
5) *The team has organizational values*
6) *The team works effectively*

The leadership continuum has the advantage of providing managers with a range of choices for involvement. It also focuses the decision maker on relevant criteria and encourages research to see how effective delegation may be under the model.

Yet this model also has some inherent limitations, most notably it involves only the initial step of assigning a task to someone. Furthermore, it works on the assumption that the manager has sufficient information on which to base decisions, and that there is a neutral environment without social bonds or politics that could potentially skew a leader's choices.

Level 5 Leadership

Level 5 leadership states that the best leaders lead from the front. They blend merciless ferocity with extreme empathy and compassion. They elicit extreme loyalty and dedication from their subordinates and always know the right people for the right job. Their egos never interfere with the ultimate goal, and they are quick to credit others and other factors for their achievements.

Steps in Level 5 Leadership Process;
1) *Hire the right people*
2) *Deploy them in the jobs which they are "intended" to do*
3) *Set a really high long-term goal*

Level 5 leadership produces excellent long-term results for the company, but it can also place grueling demands on the leader that may limit his ultimate effectiveness.

Crisis Management

No business wants to face "situations causing a significant business disruption which stimulates extensive media coverage." It can have a negative financial, political, legal and governmental impact. Substantial value destruction is to be feared especially when the crisis is not handled well in the perception of the media.

Help and Hints:
1) *Prepare contingency plans in advance*
2) *Immediately and clearly announce internally that the only person to speak about the crisis to the media is the crisis team members*
3) *Move quickly the first hours after the crisis breaks are most important*
4) *Use crisis management consultants (advice by objectivity of PR consultants is important*

5) Give accurate and correct information. Trying to manipulate information will seriously backfire

6) When deciding upon actions consider not only the short term losses but focus also on the long term effects

Executives at all level are employed to manage crises and often do so on a daily basis. The most effective management of a crisis occurs when the potential crises are detected and dealt with quickly.

In cases where the crisis has already erupted, a continuity plan is helpful to minimize the disruption and damage. One needs to identify those functions and processes that are critical to the business, then design the operation and communications contingency plans to deal with the potential failure of one or more of them and how key stakeholders will react then they find out.

Seven Habits of Leadership

This is an idea of Leadership guru Stephen Covey. It's a theory that is applicable to our personal life, our social life and our working life, but is highly applicable to leaders and managers. According to Covey our paradigms affect how we interact with others which in turn affects how they interact with us. Therefore, any effective self help program must begin with an "inside out" approach rather than looking towards our problems as being "out there." (an outside-in approach). We start by examining our own character, paradigm and motive.

The Seven Habits of Covey:

1) *Be proactive. Control one's environment, rather than the opposite. Use self determination*

2) *Begin with an end in mind. This means that the leader must be able to see the desired outcome and focus on it*

3) *Put first things first. A leader must manage his own person*

4) *Think win-win. Aim for win-win solutions for all*

5) *Seek first to understand and then be understood*

6) *Synergize. This is the habit of creative cooperation*

7) *Sharpen the saw. Learn from previous experiences and encourage this practice in others*

Achieving Organizational Excellence: What is the Forget, Borrow and Learn Framework?

According to Vijay Govindarajan and Chris Trimble in their 2005 article, "Building Breakthrough Business Within Established Organizations," a new business must forget some of what made a similar business successful, borrow those things that made the similar successful, and learn some new techniques and business practices from scratch. Note that the three challenges are complex.

- *They are present throughout new business' lifecycle*
- *They are present all at once*

- *They are related*
- *They can be at odds*
- *They need to be balanced*

The strengths of the Forget, Borrow, and Learn framework provides advice on business challenges while also decreasing resistance within the organization. The disadvantages of the framework result from its ability to address a problem but never eradicate it. The framework also decreases the need for strong leadership but never eliminates it.

Contingency Theory

Contingency theory states that the inherent dynamics of a company, a corporation and the decision –making process itself negate any predetermined leadership style. Optimizing any decision for any situation means considering all the factors of the given situation and adapting.

Contingency Theory Factors:
Some examples of such constraints (factors) include:

- *The size of the organization*
- *How the firm adapts itself to its environment*
- *Differences among resources and operations activities*
- *Assumptions of managers about employees*
- *Strategies*

Contingency also applies to leadership, organization and decision-making. Fiedler's Contingency theory is the earliest and most extensively researched. Fiedler's approach departs from trait and behavioral models by asserting that group performance is contingent on the leader's psychological orientation and on three contextual variables: group atmosphere, task structure, and leader's power position.

Expectancy Theory

The Expectancy Theory of Victor Vroom deals with motivation and management. Together with Edward Lawler and Lyman Porter, Vroom suggested that the relationship between people's behavior at work and their goals was not as simple as was first imagined by other scientists. The expectancy theory says that individuals have different sets of goals and can be motivated if they have certain expectations.

Expectancy Theory Expectations:

- *There is a positive correlation between efforts and performance*
- *Favorable performance will result in a desirable reward*
- *The reward will satisfy an important need*
- *The desire to satisfy the need is strong enough to make the effort worthwhile*

Vroom's Expectancy Theory is based upon the following three beliefs.

1. *Valence. Refers to the emotional orientations which people hold with respect to extrinsic [money, promotion, free time, benefits] or intrinsic*

[satisfaction] rewards
2. *Expectancy. Employees have different expectations and levels of confidence about what they are capable of doing*
3. *Instrumentality. The perception of employees whether they will actually receive what they desire, even if it has been promised by a manager*

Vroom suggests that an employee's beliefs about Expectancy, Instrumentality, and Valence interact psychologically. In this way they create a motivational force, such that the employee will act in a way that brings pleasure and avoids pain.

Leadership Styles

In his 2002 book "Primal Leadership," Goleman, with Richard Boyatzis and Annie McKee, introduces six leadership styles. The different leadership styles can be broken into the following categorizations:

1. *Visionary - Believes in his/her own vision*
2. *Coaching - A good listener who helps people to identify their own strengths and weaknesses*
3. *Affiliative - This is the kind of leader who promotes harmony by being friendly and empathetic*
4. *Democratic - This individual is a superb listener and a classic team player*
5. *Pacesetting - This kind of leader has a strong urge to succeed, and encourages others to follow his/her example*

6. Commanding - A leadership style best characterized by the threatening phrase, "Do it because I say so!"

Path Goal Theory

Famed Business author Robert House states in his Path Goal theory that a leader can affect his group by rewarding performance, removing obstacles to a goal, and clarifying the path to the goal. The leader must also keep in mind the situational factors that let him lead.

His subordinates must believe in his abilities. The leader must also ask his subordinates to follow his lead, that he asks them never to do anything he himself would not do. House advocates four styles of leadership:

1. *Directive Leadership. The leader gives specific guidance*
2. *Supportive Leadership. The leader is friendly and shows concern for the subordinates*
3. *Participative Leadership. The leader consults with subordinates and considers their suggestions.*
4. *Achievement-oriented Leadership. The leader sets high goals and expects subordinates to have high-level performance.*

Results Based Leadership

In their book, "Results -Based Leadership," Dave Ulrich of the University of Michigan and consultants

Jack Zenger and Norm Smallwood argue that businesses must move from thinking primarily about the inputs of leadership towards stressing the outcomes of leadership. They have developed criteria to determine if a leader is focused to achieve results. In their opinion a good leader should be:

1. *Balanced. Results balance the major dimensions of the organization (employees, organization, customers, and investors). None of the dimensions is ignored*
2. *Strategic. Results strongly link to the strategy of the firm and to its competitive position*
3. *Lasting. Results conform to both short-term and long-term goals*
4. *Selfless. Results support the whole enterprise and transcend the leader's personal gain*

Each area requires its own metrics. For employees, it is developing their human capital and commitment. For customers, providing the value they want. For investors, the goal is to reduce the costs and to let the business grow. And for the organization, it should strive to create a learning and innovative instinct.

The PAEI Model

The PAEI model (by Adizes) describes the four key roles that create a successful management team:

1. *Producer*
2. *Administrator*
3. *Entrepreneur*

4. *Integrator*

The model also states that no one person can embody the fullest of all these roles. Therefore, the ultimate management team consists of four persons. Working together, these four people will maximize each other's creativity and reach any company goal quickly and efficiently.

Ikujiro Nonaka and Hirotaka Takeuchi propose a model of the knowledge creating process to understand the dynamic nature of knowledge creation, and to manage such a process effectively:

The SECI model consists of 3 elements:

1. SECI
2. Ba
3. Knowledge Assets

SECI:

The creation of knowledge is a continuous process of dynamic interactions between tacit and explicit knowledge. The four modes of knowledge conversion interact in the spiral of knowledge creation. The spiral becomes larger in scale as it moves up through organizational levels, and can trigger new spirals of knowledge creation.

BA:

This difficult concept (there is no exact translation of the word) can be defined as a shared context in which knowledge is shared, created and utilized through interaction. An example of BA comes from the Japanese 7-11 stores in which the corporate management interacted with the local store managers, and they were able to provide a better experience for the customers.

Knowledge Assets:

These are company-specific resources that are indispensable to create values for the firm. They are the inputs, outputs, and moderating factors, of the knowledge-creating process. To effectively manage knowledge creation and exploitation, a company has to 'map' its inventory of knowledge assets. Cataloguing is however not enough: knowledge assets are dynamic; new knowledge assets can be created from existing knowledge assets.

Training within an Industry

The Training within an Industry Method was designed to hone the skills of supervisors by focusing on five specific needs.

1. *Knowledge of the Work. The information that makes an organization unique. For example: materials, machines, tools, operations, processes or technical skill*
2. *Knowledge of Responsibilities. Organization's situation regarding policies, agreements, regulations, safety rules, and interdepartmental relationships.*
3. *Skill in Instructing. Possessing knowledge and skills of the work is one thing. Being able to teach the knowledge is another in improving methods. Supervisors must make the best use of the materials,*

47

>   machines and manpower that is available
> 4. *Skill in Leading.* This helps supervisors to improve their ability to work with people and inspire workers to do their best

This method was based on four steps, which was patterned after work by Charles Allen in the First World War. Allen was an expert in adult and industrial education. He found that adults learned most successfully when there is preparation, presentation, application and testing.

Seven Surprises for New CEOs

Along with the power and authority of having the top position in an organization, there comes an avalanche of responsibility. Some new CEO's think they have done everything necessary to prepare for their new slot, but more often than not they are very quickly beset by a number of surprises. A list of the seven most common of these surprises was compiled as part of an article published by Michael Porter, Jay Lorsch and Nitin Nohria in 2004.

> 1. *You can't run the organization. The sheer volume and intensity of external demands take many by surprise. Almost every new chief executive struggles to manage the time demanded by shareholders, analysts, board members, industry groups, politicians, and other constituencies*
>
> 2. *Giving orders is very costly. No proposal should reach the CEO for final approval, unless he can*

ratify it with enthusiasm. Before then, everyone working on the matter should have raised and resolved any potential deal breakers. The CEO should be brought into the discussion only at strategically significant moments to give feedback and support

3. *It is hard to know what is really going on. Certainly, CEOs are flooded with information, but reliable information is surprisingly scarce. All information coming to the top of the enterprise is filtered, sometimes with good intentions, sometimes with not such good intentions*

4. *You are always sending a message. The words and actions of a CEO, however small or said casually, are instantly spread and amplified, scrutinized, interpreted and sometimes drastically mis-interpreted*

5. *You are not the boss. Although the CEO may sit on the top of the management hierarchy, he still reports to the board of directors. Ultimately, the board is in charge. Not the CEO*

6. *Pleasing shareholders is not the goal. CEOs must recognize that, ultimately, today's growth expectations or even the stock price are not so relevant*

7. *You are still only human. CEO should recognize that he needs connections to the world outside his organization, at home and in the community. Otherwise he risks being completely consumed by*

his corporate life

The new CEO who comes into the job expecting the unexpected, and who is prepared to be adaptable enough to meet each of these new realities, is the individual most likely to succeed in bringing greater prosperity to the company he or she now heads.

Explanation of Framing

Tversky and Kahneman founded the Framing theory, although they did not coin the term. Framing uses the idea that people make choices based on how something is presented. It is a quality of communication that leads others to accept one meaning over another. It tells not only what to think about an issue, but also how to think about that issue. Framing is found in the areas of politics, the media, religion, and negotiations. It is a necessary skill for any leader who wants success.

Framing consists of three elements: language, thought, and forethought. Language helps us to remember information and transforms the way in which we view situations. To use language, people must have thought and reflected on their own framework of interpretation and those of others. Following are Framing techniques:

1. *Metaphor:* gives a new meaning to an idea or program by comparing it to something else.
2. *Stories (myths and legends):* using an anecdote in a vivid and memorable way.

3. *Traditions (rites, rituals and ceremonies): defining an organization at regular time periods to confirm and reproduce organizational values.*
4. *Slogans, jargon and catchphrases: framing a subject in a memorable and familiar fashion.*
5. *Artifacts: illuminating corporate values through physical objects (vestiges).*
6. *Contrast: describing a subject in terms of what it is not.*
7. *Spin: speaking of a concept so as to give it a positive or negative connotation.*

Valuing Information Technology

Michael Hammer and Glenn Mangurian, in their 1987 article "The changing value of communications technology," present the Impact/Value Framework that is used to think about the value of Information Technology.

In the vertical axis is time, distance and relationships, and in the horizontal axis is efficiency (increased productivity), effectiveness (better management), and innovation (improvement in products/services). Alternatively, the benefits of Information Technology is:

1. *Strategic benefits (competitive advantage, alignment, customer relations).*
2. *Informational benefits (information access, information quality, information flexibility).*
3. *Transactional benefits (communications efficiency,*

systems development efficiency, business efficiency).

Adopting Different Leadership Styles Depending on the Situation

The Situational Leadership method from Kenneth Blanchard and Paul Hersey holds that managers must vary their leadership style depending on the employee and the situation. They characterized leadership style in terms of the amount of direction and support given by the leader. Following is a description of the four leadership behaviors:

1. *S1 – Telling/Directing: high task focus, low relationship focus – leaders supervise followers closely and make all decisions. For those with low competence, but are committed and need direction.*
2. *S2 – Selling/Coaching: high task focus, high relationship focus – leaders supervise but seek input from followers. For those who are somewhat competent but lack commitment and need direction because they are inexperienced, supports to build self-esteem, and involvement in decision-making to restore commitment.*
3. *S3 – Participating/Supporting: low task focus, high relationship focus – follower makes day-to-day decisions. For those with competence, but not confidence, and who need support to bolster confidence, but do not need much direction.*
4. *S4 – Delegating: low task focus, low relationship focus*

– decisions are made by follower. For those who are both competent and committed and need little supervision.

Leaders should be aware of which Situational Leadership style works best for them, since each leader's style must correspond to the development level of the follower. When that happens, work gets done, relationships are built up, and most importantly, the follower's development level will rise to the S4 level on the matrix, to everyone's benefit.

The process begins with an overview of each employee's tasks, followed by an assessment on each of those tasks. Then a decision is made on which leadership style would fit and this decision is discussed with the employee. A joint plan is made, followed-up, checked, and corrected, if necessary.

This model is relatively easy to understand and use. Although, the model fails to distinguish between leadership and management, and focuses too exclusively on what the person in charge does.

Exploring Different Perspectives

The Six Thinking Hats model of Edward de Bono was designed to help individuals deliberately explore a variety of perspectives on a subject. Each different-colored hat portrays a particular role. For instance, one could play devil's advocate, the black hat, if only for the sake of generating discussion. The colors of each of the six hats are:

1. *White (Observer)* – white paper, neutral; focus on information available, objective, FACTS, what is needed, how it can be obtained
2. *Red (Self, Other)* – fire, warmth; EMOTIONS, FEELINGS, intuition; presents views without explanation or justification
3. *Black (Self, Other)* – stern, judgmental, critical, why something is wrong; LOGICAL NEGATIVE view
4. *Yellow (Self, Other)* – sunshine, optimism; LOGICAL POSITIVE view looks for benefits, what's good
5. *Green (Self, Other)* – vegetation, CREATIVE thinking, possibilities and hypotheses, new ideas
6. *Blue (Observer)* – sky, cool, overview, CONTROL of PROCESS, STEPS, OTHER HATS, chairperson, organizer

A well-balanced team recognizes the need for all hats in order to consider all aspects of a problem. Using this method, individuals can speak without risk, which can improve communication, decision making, focus, and it creates an awareness of multiple perspectives for every issue. Here is an example agenda for a typical six hats workshop:

Step 1: Present the facts of the case (white hat).
Step 2: Generate ideas on how the case could be handled (green hat).

Step 3. Evaluate the merits of each idea; list benefits (yellow hat), and drawbacks (black hat).

Step 4. Get everyone's gut feeling about the alternatives (red hat).

Step 5. Summarize and adjourn the meeting (blue hat).

It is important that all members understand that wearing a hat means adopting a perspective that may not necessarily be one's own.

Understanding Giving and Receiving of Information

In the 1950s, American psychologists Joseph Luft and Harry Ingham developed the Johari Window to understand and train self-awareness for personal development, to improve communications, interpersonal relationships, group dynamics team development, and inter -group relationships. The Johari Window model represents information about a person in relation to their group, from four perspectives:

1. *Arena: what is known by the person about him/herself and is also known by others (hair color, etc.)*
2. *Blind Spot: what is unknown by the person about him/herself but what others know (how others feel about you)*
3. *Façade: what the person knows about him/herself that others do not know (secrets, hopes, desires)*
4. *The unknown: what is unknown by the person about him/herself and is also unknown by others*

The Johari Window is used for teaching and administering an understanding of:

1. How individuals communicate with themselves and others
2. How individuals present themselves to themselves and to others
3. How individuals perceive their place in the world
4. It is also suitable for multiple usage:

    1. Coaching to facilitate conversations around 'actions vs. perceived motivations'
    2. As an Organizational Development tool to visualize the political and cultural issues that may be in or out of sync within a business
    3. As a management tool to demonstrate the dynamics in a team
    4. As a self-development tool that helps to consider one's own 'behavior vs. reaction'

The Johari Window is easy to grasp, has flexible outcomes, creates a shared reference point, and encourages open information sharing. It must be remembered, though, that some things are best kept to oneself. It is a useless exercise if it is not linked to activities that reinforce positive behavior or correct negative behaviors.

Chapter – 3 Marketing and Branding

"You can have brilliant ideas, but if you can not get them across, your ideas will not get you anywhere" - Lee Iacocca

Brand Personality Model

To build customer identification with a product, marketers sometimes want to link the product with "personality traits" that customers will easily relate to. This is called the Brand Personality Model. Let's take, for example, automobiles. Even a casual observation of car advertising on TV suggests that the manufacturers are convinced that the reasons people buy one particular vehicle over another are deeply rooted in the buyer's personality. They see the car they drive as an extension of their own personality, a reflection of who they are. The Brand Personality Model describes five "dimensions of personality." These are:

1. *Sincerity*
2. *Excitement*
3. *Competence*
4. *Sophistication*
5. *Ruggedness*

Think how easily our allusion to automobiles can fit it into any of these dimensions. Some vehicles, for example, readily connote the dimension of "excitement." Sports cars quickly come to mind. "Sophistication," on the other hand, evokes images of luxury cars, high end, expensive transportation that appeals to people who like to think of themselves as upper class and charming (two of the facets of that particular dimension).

Now, this form of branding does come with some caveats. For example, a person might have the personality traits the manufacturer is targeting, but has not yet attained enough status in life to afford his dream car. So the middle class consumer who dreams of a "sophisticated" luxury car probably won't actually be in a position to buy it anytime soon. Of course, in such a case this particular buyer is likely to identify with a competing product that also has a certain personal appeal to him. Perhaps "competence," which suggests reliability. This would be very important to a person whose limited budget needs to take into consideration practical things such as gas mileage and infrequent repairs.

Each one of these five "dimensions of personality" has been carefully researched. The end result, when coupled with appropriate advertising, is that the buyer will indeed get the message the manufacturer is sending -- and respond to it. This can be true not only for cars, but across the spectrum of products and brands that are marketed to the public. Moreover, the Brand Personality Model is a useful tool for assessing the current status of a brand, and to describe the desired future status of the brand.

Extended Marketing

Booms and Bitner developed a marketing strategy tool that expands the number of controllable variables from the four in the original Marketing Mix Model to seven. These additional variables make the expanded model more useful for service oriented industries rather than for tangible products. They are also helpful when dealing with knowledge intensive environments. The three extra variables can be briefly described as follows:

1. *People - everyone involved is an important part of the extended Marketing Mix. Knowledge, Workers, Employees, Management and other Consumers often add significant value to the total product or serve*

2. *Process procedure, mechanisms and flow of activities by which services are consumed (customer management processes) are an essential element of the marketing strategy*

3. *Physical Evidence – the ability and environment in which the service is delivered, both tangible goods that help to communicate and perform the service and the intangible experience of existing customers and the ability of the business to relay that customer satisfaction to potential Customers*

This expanded strategy, its proponents argue, also involves the accessibility of the service as well as the input of front-line service personnel.

Measuring Brand Value

The advertising agency Young and Rubicam

developed the brand asset valuator by applying four broad factors:

1. *Differentiation - the ability for a brand to be distinguished from its competitors*

2. *Relevance - the actual and perceived importance of the brand to a large consumer market segment*

3. *Esteem - the perceived quality and consumer perceptions about the growing or declining Popularity of a brand*

4. *Knowledge - the extent of the consumer's awareness of the brand and understanding of its identity*

The data for the brand asset valuator comes from a far – reaching survey that asked questions of over 230,000 respondents in 44 countries regarding approximately 20,000 brands.

Dominating Your Industry

Every industry has its leaders. These are usually giant companies that have become household names. The Rule of Three method developed by Jagdish Sheth and Rajendra Sisodia holds that three big companies will evolve/adapt to dominate any industry. You can easily see it. For instance, McDonalds, Burger King and Wendy's would exemplify this phenomenon in the fast food industry. Typically, the competitors eventually emerge to capture between seventy to ninety percent of a given market. Accordingly, this is a useful strategy for understanding competitive moves in businesses, small or large.

This strategy, however, has certain limitations. For example, there can be exceptions to it, which are not easily explained. Also, other factors may influence the number and dominance of market players. Some say there is nothing "magic" about the number 3, and the actual number of companies that will dominate in any given industry will be determined by the way in which the government enforces anti - trust laws.

Blue Ocean Strategy

Rather than competing within the confines of the existing industry (Bloody or Red Ocean Strategy) W. Chan Kim and Renée Mauborgne are suggesting Blue Ocean Strategy: developing uncontested market space that makes the competition irrelevant.

Two Ways to Create Blue Oceans:

1) *One is to launch completely new industries, as eBay did with online auctions*
2) *It is more common for a blue ocean to be created from within a red ocean when a company expands the boundaries of an existing industry*

Competitive Advantages

According to the Competitive Advantage model of Michael Porter, a competitive strategy takes offensive or defensive action to create a defendable position in an industry, in order to cope successfully with competitive forces and generate a superior return on investment.

Overview of the Book "Competitive Strategy"

In Part I, Porter discuss the structural analysis of industries, offering an excellent framework for competitor analysis, competitive moves, strategy toward buyers and suppliers, structural analysis within industries, and industry evolution. In Part II, Porter discusses competitive strategy within various generic industry environments, such as: fragmented industries (with no real market leader), emerging industries, mature industries, declining industries, and global industries. In Part III, Porter discusses strategic decisions that businesses/firms can take, such as: vertical integration (forward, backward, partnerships), capacity expansion, and entry into new industries/businesses.

Competitive Forces

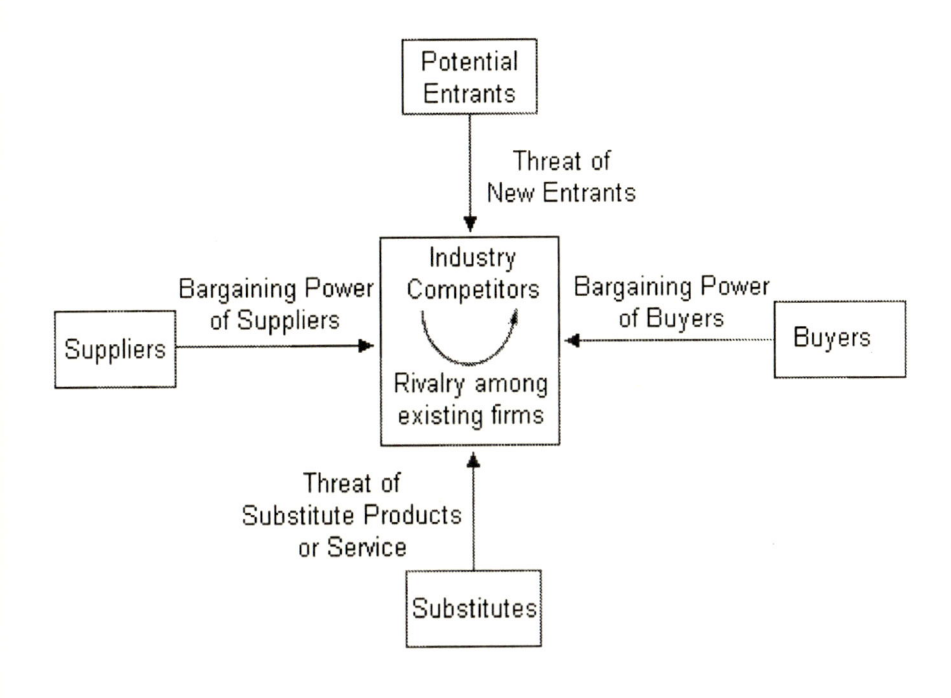

Figure 3.1

The Five Forces model of Porter identifies five fundamental competitive forces:

1. *Entry of competitors. How easy or difficult is it for new entrants to start competing*
2. *Threat of substitutes. How easy can a product or service be substituted, especially made cheaper*
3. *Bargaining power of buyers. How strong is the position of buyers? Can they work together in ordering large volumes*
4. *Bargaining power of suppliers. How strong is the position of sellers? Do many potential suppliers*

exist or only few potential suppliers?

5. *Rivalry among the existing players. Does a strong competition exist between the current entities?*

Porter's Competitive Forces model is probably one of the most often used business strategy tools.

Marketing Mix

The Marketing Mix model can be used by marketers as a tool to implement marketing strategy. Marketing managers use this method to generate the optimal response in the target market by blending 4, 5, or 7 variables in an optimal way.

Product	Historically, the thinking was: a good product will sell itself. Define the characteristics of your product or service that meets the needs of your customers.	Functionality; Quality; Appearance; Packaging; Brand; Service; Support; Warranty.

Price	How much are the customers willing to pay? Although competition in the market place plays a big factor, the consumer remains sensitive to price discounts and special offers. Price has also an irrational side: something that is expensive must be good.	List Price; Discounts; Financing; Leasing Options; Allowances.
Place	Is the product or service available at the right place, at the right time, in the right quantities? Think of the Internet and mobile telephones.	Locations; Logistics; Channel members; Channel Motivation; Market Coverage; Service Levels; Internet; Mobile.
Promotion	How are the target groups informed or educated about the organization and its products? This includes all the weapons in the marketing armory - advertising, selling, sales.	Advertising; Public Relations; Message; Direct Sales; Sales; Media; Budget.

Figure 3.2

The function of the Marketing Mix is to help develop a package (mix) that will not only satisfy the needs of the customers within the target markets, but simultaneously to maximize the performance of the organization.

The Diamond Model

The Diamond Model of Michael Porter offers a model that can illustrate the relative position of a nation in global competition. The model can also be used for major geographic regions

Traditionally, economic theory mentions the following factors for comparative advantage for regions or countries:

1) *Land*
2) *Location*
3) *Natural resources (minerals, energy)*
4) *Labor, and*
5) *Local population size.*

Interlinked Advanced Factors For Competitive Advantage:

1. *The Strategy, Structure and Rivalry of Firms. The world is dominated by dynamic conditions. Direct competition compels firms to work for increases in productivity and innovation*
2. *Demand Conditions. If the customers in an economy are very demanding, the pressure facing firms to constantly improve their competitiveness*
3. *Related Supporting Industries. Spatial proximity of upstream or downstream industries facilitates the exchange of information and promotes a continuous exchange of ideas and innovations*

4. *Factor Conditions. Contrary to conventional wisdom, Porter argues that the "key" factors of production are created, not inherited. Specialized factors of production are skilled labor, capital and infrastructure. "Non-key" factors or general use factors, such as unskilled labor and raw materials can be obtained by any company and, hence, do not generate sustained competitive advantage*

In the Diamond Model, the role of government a catalyst and challenger; it is to encourage - or even push- companies to higher levels of competitive performance.

Brand Identity

According to Jean-Noël Kapferer, brand personality should be just one key facet of brand identity. Brand personality has three distinct characteristics.

1) *Physical. What does the product do and how well does it perform?*
2) *Character. Brand personality facet*
3) *Style. Operational elements for adverting and communication*

Analogously to the use of the term "personality" in psychology, on the research side, the brand identity frameworks always quoted brand personality as a dimension of brand identity.

Customer Satisfaction

The customer satisfaction model from N. Kano is a quality management and marketing technique that can be used for measuring client happiness. Kano's model of customer satisfaction distinguishes six categories of quality attributes, from which the first three actually influence customer satisfaction.

1. *Basic Factors. The minimum requirements that will cause dissatisfaction if they are not fulfilled. The customer regards these as prerequisites and takes these for granted*
2. *Excitement Factors. The factors that increase customer satisfaction if delivered but do not cause dissatisfaction if they are not delivered*
3. *Performance Factors. The factors that cause satisfaction if the performance is high and they cause dissatisfaction if the performance is low*
4. *Indifferent attributes. The customer does not care about this feature*
5. *Questionable attributes. It is unclear whether this attribute is expected by the customer*
6. *Reverse attributes. The reverse of this product feature was expected by the customer*

Distinctive Capabilities

In "Foundations of Corporate Success", John Kay argues that the best businesses derive their strength from a distinctive structure of relationships with employees, customers, and suppliers. According to John Kay, there are three Distinctive Capabilities that a company can employ to create added value and achieve competitive advantage through relationships:

1. *Architecture. A structure of relational contacts within or around the organization with employees and with customers and suppliers*
2. *Reputation. Built up through:*
   1. *Customer's own experience*
   2. *Consistent quality*
   3. *Demonstrations and free trials*
   4. *Warranty*
   5. *Guarantee*
   6. *Word of mouth*
   7. *Association with other brands*
   8. *Staking the reputation once it is established*
3. *Innovation. Provided the innovation is translated to competitive advantage successfully*

Strategic Triangle

Strategic Triangle: used for defining strategic positions that reflects new sources of profitability. Three strategic options: best product, customer solutions, and system lock -in. Three fundamental processes are always present and are the repository of key strategic tasks: operational effectiveness, customer targeting, and innovation.

The Delta Model identifies the core processes of the business and provides a guide for the unique function of each process to achieve different strategic positions capable of continually responding to an uncertain environment.

Value Net

Successful business strategy means actively shaping the game you play, not just shaping the game you find. Managers can benefit by using the insights from game theory to design a game that is right for their companies. The rewards that can come from changing a game may be far greater than those from maintaining the status quo. Sometimes the best way to succeed is to let others be successful, including your competitors.

Win-lose strategies often have negative effects. The game of business is to create and to capture value. The Value Net is a schematic map designed to represent all the players in the game and the interdependencies among them.

The Value Net model from Adam Brandenburger and Barry Nalebuff recognizes four main groups that influence any firm:

1. *Customers*
2. *Suppliers*
3. *Competitors*
4. *Complements*

In addition to analyzing the competitive market, this model focuses the analysis of the forces in adjacent and related markets that must be monitored because the company relies on their product being available.

Clicks and Mortar

The Clicks and Mortar business model refers to the marriage of traditional ways of conducting business (often using direct, face-to-face contacts with customers) and the Internet to interact with customers (often via websites, email, FTP and other internet technologies). The integration of e-commerce with existing physical channels is a challenging undertaking that can create problems for management. Marketing theorists have long recognized the potential for channel conflicts that can occur when products can take alternative paths to the end consumer.

The Clicks and Mortar business model suggests that traditional sales channels can be operated along or even in an integrated way with Internet sales channels. The Clicks and Mortar model offers an advantage of integrating the physical and online channels enabling firms to capitalize on potential synergies between the two, yielding competitive advantages over pure internet firms. Pure dotcoms, on the other hand, have an advantage in areas that stress cost efficiency. They are not burdened with Brick and Mortar costs and can offer products at very low marginal cost. However, they sometimes spend substantially more on customer acquisition.

Economic Margin

The Economic Margin framework of Daniel J. Obrycki and Rafael Resendes calculates the competition adjusted corporate performance.

Economic Cash Flow Perspective:

The Economic Margin (EM) framework evaluates corporate performance. It corrects for distortions accounting-based analysis that were caused by the following differences: capital structure, asset age, asset life, asset mix, off-balance-sheet assets and liabilities, and the investment which is needed to generate earnings and cost of capital.

Unlike many traditional valuation approaches that utilize highly sensitive eternity assumptions, the Economic Margin approach follows the widely accepted economic principle that its competitors will equalize excess returns over time.

The Economic Margin framework is grounded in the widely agreed theories of Nobel price winning Merton Miller and Franco Modigliani. EM can help to identify companies trading above or below their intrinsic valuations.

Experience Curve Effect

First described by Bruce Henderson in 1960, the Experience Curve Effect states that if a task is performed more often, the cost of performing the task will decrease. Researchers since then have observed experience curve effects for various industries ranging between 10 to 30 percent.

If a company can gain a big market share quickly in a new market, it has a competitive cost advantage because it can produce products cheaper than its competitors. Provided the cost savings are passed on to the buyers as price decreases, the company can sustain its advantage. If a company can accelerate its production experience by increasing its market share, it then can gain a cost advantage in its industry that would be hard to equal. The result is many companies try to gain a large market share quickly by investing heavily and aggressively pricing their products or services in new markets. Rapid growth must be kept in proportion to revenues generated, and the company must be careful about incurring debt in expansion. The debt may be a valuable investment and can be recovered later, once the company has become a market leader.

Exploratory Factor Analysis

First identified in 1904 and later modified in the 1930's, Exploratory Factor Analysis distills underlying factors from large volumes of data. Using the data mined from questionnaires, the method filters trends and generalities that can be very useful to managers as they work to improve interactions with customers, buyers, and workers.

Usage of Exploratory Factor Analysis Applications:

- *Customer satisfaction surveys*
- *Measuring service quality*
- *Personality tests*
- *Image surveys*
- *Identifying market segments*
- *Typing customers or products or behavior*

The Exploratory Factor Analysis can be used in a wide variety of applications with large amounts of data. It requires competent users and managers who can apply the results of the analysis.

Resource Based View

The Resource Based View holds that firms can earn sustainable supra-normal returns if and only if they have superior resources and some form of isolating mechanism preventing their diffusion throughout industry protects those resources. Most scholars consider Jay Barney as the father of the modern Resource-Based View of the Firm (RBV). The RBV emphasizes strategic choice, charging the management of the firm with the important tasks of identifying, developing and deploying key resources to maximize returns.

Differences may occur in the form of resources such as patents, properties, proprietary technologies, or relationships. A study by Danny Miller of a number of firms shows how some of them were able to build not so much on resources and capabilities as on asymmetries. Asymmetries are typically skills, processes, or assets a firm's competitors do not and cannot copy at a cost that affords economic rents. Often these asymmetries act as liabilities, but by embedding them within a complementary organizational design, and leveraging them across appropriate market opportunities, many firms were able to turn asymmetries into sustainable capabilities.

Chapter 4 - Human Resources Strategy

"If an institution wants to be adaptive, it has to let go of some control and trust that people will work on the right things in the right way" - Robert B. Shapiro, CEO of chemical company Monsanto in Harvard Business Review, Jan –Feb 1997

Changing Behavior

This theory was espoused by Icek Aizen. It helps to understand how we can change behavior of people. The TPB is a theory that predicts deliberate behavior, since behavior can be planned.

Three TPB Considerations:

1. *Behavioral Beliefs: The consequences of behavior that produces a favorable or unfavorable attitude about the behavior*

2. *Normative Beliefs: These are about the normative expectations of others and results in perceived social pressure*

3. *Control Beliefs: These are beliefs about the presence of factors that may facilitate or may impede the performance of the behavior. As a general rule, if the attitude and subjective norm are more favorable the perceived control will be greater and the persons*

intention to perform the behavior in question should be stronger.

Cultural Dimensions

This is a theory by Geert Ho fstede maintaining that there is no such thing as a universal management method or theory that is valid worldwide. The Five Cultural Dimensions describe five sorts of differences/value perspectives between national cultures:

1. *Power Distance -- The degree of inequality considered normal by any culture*

2. *Individualism versus collectivism -- The extent to which people feel that they are supposed to take care of themselves*

3. *Masculinity vs. femininity -- The extent to which a culture is conducive to dominance and assertiveness*

4. *Uncertainty avoidance -- The degree to which people prefer structured situations*

5. *Long-term versus short-term orientation. -- Long-term values are oriented towards the future, like saving and persistence. Short-term values are oriented d towards the past and present, like respect for tradition and fulfilling social obligations*

To understand management in a country, one should have knowledge and empathy with the local scene. All cultures are bound to be different. People act and react based on their own experiences.

ERG Theory

Clayton P Alderfer's model that appeared in a 1969 Psychological Review article entitled "An Empirical Test of a New theory of Human Need." Alderfer distinguishes three categories of human needs that influence a worker's behavior, existence, relatedness and growth.

The ERG Categories of Human Needs:
1. *Existence. Self preservation*
2. *Relatedness Needs. Social and external esteem*
3. *Growth Needs. Internal esteem and self actualization (need to be creative, productive)*

Another aspect of the theory involves the Frustration/ regression principle, which states that if a higher level need remains unfulfilled, the person may regress towards lower level needs, which are easier to satisfy. This principle impacts workplace motivation. In other words, if growth opportunities are not offered the employee may regress towards relatedness needs, and socialize more with co -workers.

Dimensions of Relational Work

According to Butler and Waldroop, interpersonal common sense is critical in almost any area of business. Basically, managers can boost productivity by hiring the right employees, making the best work assignments, rewarding performance and promoting career development.

One key dimension of relational work is to influence people. Professionals enjoy developing and extending their sphere of interpersonal influence They like to negotiate and persuade and the power of ideas.

Interpersonal facilitation is done by people who are keenly attuned to the interpersonal aspect of work situations. They intuitively focus on others' experiences and usually keep their colleagues committed and engaged to the benefit of the organization. The relational creativity comes from people who are good at making connections with groups of people through visual and verbal imagery.

The authors also emphasize team leadership. This involves people who want to see other people and interact with them. They like managing and working in high energy teams in hectic service environments.

Of course, many of these people can have great interest and skill in two or more areas or in none of them. But all types of relational work contribute to the bottom line and should be rewarded (which can involve either monetary or non monetary rewards.

Total Quality Management

Edward Deming was an American statistician who is associated with the rise of Japan as a manufacturing nation and with the invention of Total Quality Management. Deming returned to the US and published a book, "Out of the Crisis." In the book he set out 14 points which, he believed, if applied to the US manufacturing industry, would save the US from industrial doom by the Japanese. Here is a summary of Deming's 14 points of management:

1. Create constancy of purpose for improvement of product

and service. Companies need to allocate resources for long term planning, research and education

2. Adopt the new philosophy. Government regulations representing obstacles must be removed.
3. End the practice of awarding business on the basis of price tags alone. Need long term relationships with single suppliers
4. End the dependence on mass inspections. Prevent defects instead of trying to detect and fix them
5. Improve constantly and forever the system of production and service
6. Institute training
7. Adopt and institute leadership. Managers should lead, not supervise
8. Drive out fear. Make employees feel secure enough to express ideas and ask questions
9. Break down barriers between staff areas. Teams will solve many problems
10. Eliminate numerical quotas for the workforce and numerical goals for management
11. Eliminate slogans, warnings and targets for the workforce. Most generate resentment rather than inspiration
12. Remove barriers that rob people of pride of workmanship
13. Encourage education and self improvement for everyone
14. Take action to accomplish the transformation; commitment needed by employees and management

European Form Quality Management

The European Form Quality Management model recognizes many approaches to achieving sustainable excellence. Within this non-prescriptive approach there are some fundamental concepts that underpin the EFQM Model. The EFQM Model recognizes that there are many approaches to achieving sustainable excellence in all aspects of performance.

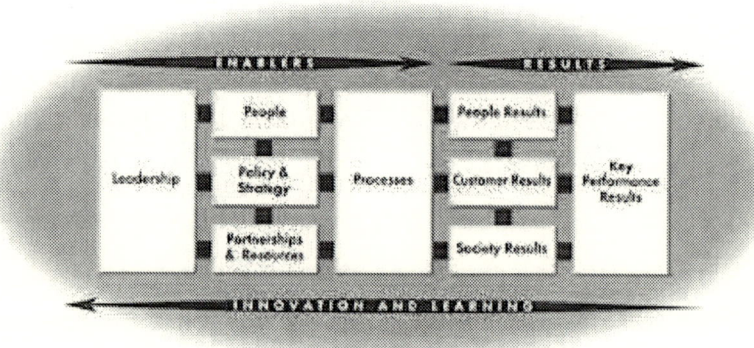

Figure 4.1

This model is based on the assumption that excellent results with respect to performance, customers, people and society are achieved through Leadership driving policy and strategy that is delivered through people, partnerships and resources, and processes.

The EFQM Model is a non-prescriptive Total Quality Management framework based on nine criteria. Five of these are 'Enablers' and four are 'Results'. The 'Enabler' criteria are covering what an organization does. The 'Results' criteria are covering what an organization achieves. 'Results' are caused by 'Enablers' and feedback from 'Results' help to improve 'Enablers'.

People Capability Maturity Model (PCMM)

The People Capability Maturity Model (People CMM) framework, maintained by the Carnegie Mellon SEI, organizes the maturity of their workforce, and addresses their critical people issues. P-CMM can guide organizations to improve their processes for managing and developing their workforces.

People CMM provides a roadmap for implementing workforce practices that continuously improve the capability of an organization's workforce

Five Stages of the People C MM Framework

1. *Initial Level. Typical characteristics: Inconsistency in performing practices.*
2. *Managed Level. Typical characteristics: Work overload, Environmental distractions, unclear performance objectives or feedback.*
3. *Defined Level. Although the basic workforce practices are implemented, the organization misses opportunities to standardize workforce practices.*
4. *Predictable Level. The organization manages and exploits the capability created by its framework of workforce competencies.*
5. *Optimizing Level. The entire organization is focused on continual improvement.*

Cultural Intelligence

Cultural Intelligence is the ability to cope with national, corporate and vocational cultures as described by Christopher Earley and Elaine Mosakowski in the Harvard Business Review of October 2004. Cultural Intelligence is the ability to understand unfamiliar contexts, and then to adjust. The following are the three sources of cultural intelligence:

1. *The Head / Cognitive. Rote learning of the beliefs, habits and taboos of foreign cultures,*
2. *The Body / Physical. Your actions and demeanor must prove that you have entered their world.*
3. *The Heart / Emotional/motivational. To adjust to a new culture involves overcoming obstacles and setbacks. People can do that only if they believe in their own efficacy.*

In an increasingly diverse business environment, managers must be able to navigate through the thickest of habits, gestures, and assumptions that define their coworkers' differences. Foreign cultures appear not only in other countries but also in corporations and regions.

Emotional Intelligence

Since the late 1930's, researchers have found that pure intelligence alone plays only a partial factor in determining an individual's overall performance. The factor of emotional intelligence, the ability to understand the monitoring and reaction to one's own feelings and those of others, will determine the total performance potential of an individual.

Trained as a psychologist at Harvard, Daniel Goleman wrote the popular bestseller "Emotional Intelligence" (1995), in which he offered the first proof that emotional and social factors are important. There are five domains of emotional intelligence:

1. *Knowing one's emotions. Self-awareness, recognizing a feeling while it happens.*
2. *Managing emotions. The ability to handle feelings so they are appropriate.*
3. *Motivating one. Marshalling emotions in the service of a goal.*
4. *Recognizing emotions in others. Empathy, social awareness.*
5. *Handling relationships. Skill in managing emotions of others.*

According to Goleman, these Emotional Intelligent competencies are not innate talents. They are learned abilities.

Organizational Configuration

The organizational configurations framework of Mintzberg describes six valid organizational setups. See Figure 4.2 below.

Six Basic Parts of the Organization

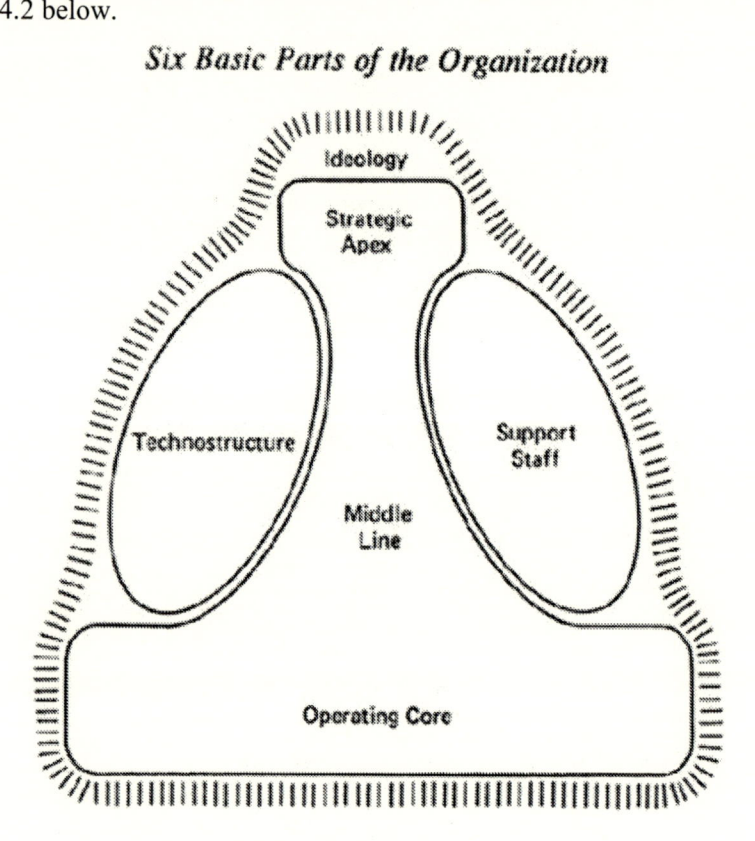

Figure 4.2

Valid Organizational Configurations

1. *Entrepreneurial*
2. *Machine*
3. *Professional*
4. *Diversified*
5. *Innovative*
6. *Missionary*

(See further explanation below for Entrepreneurial, Machine, and Professional and Innovative organizational configurations).

1. The Entrepreneurial Startup (The Simple Structure)

Typically, the start-up has little or no techno structure, few support staffers, a loose division of labor, minimal differentiation among its units, and a small managerial hierarchy. Little of its behavior is formalized, and it makes minimal use of planning, training, and liaison devices.

2. The Machine Bureaucracy

The machine bureaucracy depends primarily on the standardization of its operating work processes for coordination. Because of that, the techno structure, which houses the analysts who do the standardizing, emerges as the key part of the structure. It features research: highly specialized, routine operating tasks; much formalized procedures in the operating core; a proliferation of rules, regulations, and formalized communication throughout the organization.

Machine bureaucratic work is found in environments that are simple and stable. The work of complex environments cannot be rationalized into simple tasks, and that of dynamic environments cannot be predicted, made repetitive, and so standardized.

3. The Professional Bureaucracy

The professional bureaucracy relies on the standardization of skills and its associated design parameter, training and indoctrination. It hires duly trained and indoctrinated specialists.

5. The Adhocracy (Innovation)

Unlike the professional bureaucracy, the adhocracy cannot rely on the standardized skills of these experts to achieve coordination because that would cause standardization instead of innovation. Rather, it must treat existing knowledge and skills merely as a basis on which to build new ones.

Managers abound in the adhocracy - functional managers, integrating managers, project managers. The last named are particularly numerous, since the project teams must be small to encourage mutual adjustment among their members, and each team needs a designated leader, a "manager." Managers become functioning members of project teams, with special responsibility to effect coordination between them. The adhocracy can take two basic forms:

5a. The Operating Adhocracy

The operating adhocracy innovates and solves problems directly on behalf of its clients. Its multidisciplinary teams of experts often work under contract, as in the think-tank consulting firm, creative advertising agency, or manufacturer of engineering prototypes.

5b. The Administrative Adhocracy

The second type of adhocracy also functions with project teams but toward a different purpose. Whereas the operating adhocracy undertakes projects to serve its clients, the administrative adhocracy undertakes projects to serve itself, to bring new facilities or activities on line, as in the administrative structure of a highly automated company. And in sharp contrast to the operating adhocracy, the administrative adhocracy makes a clear distinction between its administrative component and its operating core. The core is truncated - cut off from the rest of the organization - so that the administrative component that remains can be structured as an adhocracy.

Spiral Dynamics

Clare Graves expressed Spiral Dynamics as the psychology of the mature human being an unfolding, emergent, oscillating, spiraling process marked by progressive subordination of older, lower -order behavior systems to newer, higher-order systems as man's existential problems change. And more comprehensively, at each stage of human existence the adult male is off on his quest of his holy grail, the way of life he seeks by which to live.

At his first level he is on a quest for automatic physiological satisfaction. At the second level he seeks a safe mode of living, and this is followed by a search heroic status, for power and glory, by a search for ultimate peace. His search then continues for material pleasure and affectionate relations then for respect of self and for peace in an incomprehensible world. When he discovers that he will not find that peace, he will be off on his ninth level quest. Every stage he reaches leaves him disconcerted and perplexed. It is simply that while he solves one set of human problems he finds a new set in their place. The spiral ever continues, like a circle in a circle or a wheel within a wheel.

The Theory X Theory and Theory Y Theory

Douglas McGregor, an American social psychologist, proposed his famous Theory X and Theory Y models in his book, 'The Human Side of Enterprise' (1960). See Figure 4.3 below.

	Theory X	**Theory Y**
Assumptions	Humans inherently dislike working and will try to avoid it if they can.	People view work as being as natural as play and rest. Humans expend the same amount of physical and mental effort in their work as in their private lives.
	Because people dislike work they have to be coerced or controlled by management and threatened so they work hard enough.	Provided people are motivated, they will be self-directing to the aims of the organization. Control and punishment are not the only mechanisms to let people perform.
	Average employees want to be directed.	Job satisfaction is key to engaging employees and ensuring their commitment.
	People don't like	People learn to accept

	responsibility.	responsibility and seek responsibility. Average humans, under the proper conditions, will not only accept, but even naturally seek responsibility.
	Average humans are clear and unambiguous and want to feel secure at work.	People are imaginative and creative. Their ingenuity should be used to solve problems at work.
Application	Shop Floor, Mass Manufacturing. Production workers.	Professional Services, Knowledge Workers. Managers and Professionals.
Conducive	Large scale efficient operations.	Management of Professionals, Participative Complex Problem Solving.
Management Style	Authoritarian, Hard Management.	Participative, Soft Management.

Figure 4.3

McGregor sees Theory Y as the preferable model and management method, however he thought Theory Y was difficult to use in large-scale operations.

The Two Factor Theory

According to the Two Factor Theory of Frederick Herzberg people are influenced by satisfaction and dissatisfaction Herzberg developed this motivation theory during his investigation of 200 accountants and engineers in the USA. The two factors are:

1. *Corporate Hygiene factors are needed to ensure that an employee does not become dissatisfied. They do not cause higher levels of motivation, but without them there is dissatisfaction.*
2. *Motivation factors are needed in order to motivate an employee into higher performance. These factors result from internal generators in employees.*

Here is a breakdown of typical corporate hygiene factors:

- *Working conditions*
- *Quality of supervision*
- *Salary*
- *Status*
- *Safety*
- *Company*
- *Job*
- *Company policies and administration*

- *Interpersonal relations*

…and here are some typical motivation factors:
- *Achievement*
- *Recognition for achievement*
- *Responsibility for task*
- *Interesting job*
- *Advancement to higher level tasks*
- *Growth*

Besides The Two Factor Theory, Frederick Herzberg is also known for his acronym KITA, which has been politely translated as a Kick In The Pants! Herzberg said that KITA does not produce motivation, only movement.

Chapter 5 - Decision-making and Valuation

"Everything that can be counted does not necessarily count; everything that counts cannot necessarily be counted" - Albert Einstein 1879 -1955, German- born American theoretical physicist

Management Buy-out

Essentially, an MBO is the purchase of a business by its existing management, usually in cooperation with outside financiers. Managers acquire equities in their business, sometimes a controlling stake, for a relatively modest personal investment. To be successful the management team should be well balanced, the business must be commercially viable, the vendor willing and the price realistic.

Reasons:
1. Certain parts of an organization are no longer seen as no core activity by its parent company.
2. A company is in financial distress.
3. Parts of acquisitions that are not wanted.
4. In case of a family business: succession issuers through retirement of the owner.
5. The management team wants to gain independence and autonomy.

Attractiveness of the MBO to a seller:

1. Speed. Much quicker than a trade sale.
2. Strategic considerations. Wish to keep the business out of competition's hands.
3. Confidentiality. Do not want sensitive info to get out.

4. *Familiarity.* With an MBO the selling party can continue to deal with the management team.

Typical steps in a MBO process:

1. *Agreement on officers, financial consultants, auditors and investors.*
2. *Evaluation of the selling price.*
3. *Formulation of business plans.*
4. *Obtaining finance.*

Using Analogies to Make Strategic Choices

Explaining the concept of analogical strategic reasoning is credited to Giovanni Gavetti and Jan W. Rivkin. Faced with an unfamiliar problem, senior managers often will reflect on similar situations they have experienced or witnessed, draw lessons from it, and then apply those lessons to the present situation.

Application:

Analogical strategic reasoning can be used as a tool to choose between possible solutions to strategic problems. It is also useful as a catalyst for generating creative options. And it can communicate complex messages quickly, as people understand simple analogies.

Benefits:

Compared to deduction and trial and error, analogical strategic reasoning has the advantage because problems are not so complex that only trial and error can solve them, nor are they so familiar that they permit deduction. The amount of information available in many strategic situations is similar to the information required to draw analogies. The wealth of managerial experience matches the need for that experience in analogical reasoning. Also the need for creative strategies can be fulfilled through analogy's ability to spark creativity.

Limitations:

The danger exists of drawing an analogy on the basis of a similarity that is too superficial, not one with deep causal traits. Distinguishing deep similarities from superficial resemblances is difficult. People tend to make little effort to draw such distinctions. This is caused by anchoring, which means that once an analogy is used, it tends to anchor itself and is hard to dislodge. It is also caused by confirmation bias on the part of decision makers, who are inclined to seek out information confirming their beliefs and ignore contradicting data.

To avoid these pitfalls, the following four steps are recommended:

1. *Recognize the analogy and identify its purpose. Is analogy being used and how?*
2. *Understand the source. Why did the strategy work in a former situation?*
3. *Assess similarity. Is the similarity more than superficial? Where are the differences?*
4. *Translate, decide and adapt. Will the properly translated analogy work in the target industry?*

Searching for Excellent Organizations

The Eight Attributes of Management Excellence of Tom Peters and Bob Waterman were described in their book, "In Search of Excellence," based on the McKinsey 7-S Model. Listed below are the eight attributes:

1. *A bias for action.*
2. *Close to the customer.*
3. *Autonomy and entrepreneurship.*
4. *Productivity through people.*
5. *Hands-on, value-driven.*
6. *Stick to the knitting.*
7. *Simple form, lean staff.*
8. *Simultaneous loose-tight properties – this attribute is, in fact, a summary of the previous seven. Organizations that live by this attribute are, on the one hand, rigidly controlled, yet at the same time insist on autonomy, entrepreneurship, and innovation from the rank and file, according to Peters and Waterman.*

Peters said that a ninth attribute should be added to the above list: This ninth attribute involve capabilities concerning ideas, liberation, and speed.

Studying How People Interact and Make Decisions by Applying Mathematical Models

Game Theory, a special branch of mathematics, has been developed for studying decision-making in complex circumstances. Whereas this idea has deep historical roots, its modern codification has been attributed to John von Neumann, Oskar Morgenstern, and John Nash.

Game Theory applies mathematical models to interactions between people with the assumption that each person's behavior impacts the well-being of all other participants in the game. This need to make assumptions is one of the major issues with game theory. There are two assumptions that usually arise:

1. *Rationality: People will take whatever actions are likely to make them happier.*
2. *Common knowledge: Each person tries to make himself happier, potentially at our expense.*

Probably the most widely known example of this theory is the prisoner's dilemma. Two prisoners, suspected of collaborating in a crime, are arrested. There is not enough evidence to convict either of them, so the prisoners are isolated from each other and each offered a deal. If either one of them gives evidence against the other, they go free. If neither one of them does so, both of them will get some sort of punishment. Here's where the assumption comes in – neither of the prisoners know what the other will do.

Adjusting the Strategy and Structure of Organizations While They Develop

The 1972 Growth Phases Model of Greiner describes five phases of organizational development and growth. This model can be used to understand why some management styles and organizational structures work, and some do not.

1. *Growth through creativity. Start-up company, entrepreneurial, informal communication, hard work - low earnings. Ending by a leadership crisis.*

2. *Growth through direction. Sustained growth, functional structure, accounting, capital management, incentives, and budgets. Ending by an autonomy crisis.*
3. *Growth through delegation. Decentralized structure, market level responsibility, profit centers, financial incentives, decision making based on periodic reviews, top management acts by exception, formal communication. Ending by a control crisis.*
4. *Growth through coordination and monitoring. Formation of product groups, thorough review of formal planning, centralization of support functions, corporate staff oversees coordination, corporate capital expenditures, and accountability for ROI at product Group level, motivation through lower -level profit sharing. Ending by a red tape crisis.*
5. *Growth through collaboration. Team action for problem solving, cross -functional task teams, decentralized support staff, matrix organization, simplified control mechanisms, team behavior education programs, and advanced information systems, team incentives. Ending by an internal growth crisis.*

Greiner has recently added a sixth phase, the growth through extra-organizational solutions. These would include mergers, holdings, and networks of organizations.

Conscious, Step-by-step Approach to Complete Decision-making

The Kepner-Tregoe Matrix is a step -by-step approach to systematically solving problems, making good decisions, and analyzing potential risks and opportunities. It is a structured methodology for identifying and ranking all factors critical to a decision, and is used mainly to limit biases that tend to obscure a decision's primary objectives. This approach can be applied to nearly all decisions, ranging from product marketing to site selection. The following are the steps involved in utilizing the Kepner-Tregoe approach:

1. *Prepare a decision statement that includes both an action and a result.*
2. *Establish strategic requirements (Musts), operational objectives (Wants), and restraints (Limits).*
3. *Rank each objective and assign relative weights.*
4. *Generate alternatives.*
5. *Assign a relative score for each alternative on an objective-by-objective basis.*
6. *Calculate weighted score for each alternative and identify top two or three.*
7. *List adverse consequences for each top alternative and evaluate probability (high, medium, low) and severity (high, medium, and low).*
8. *Make a final, single choice between top alternatives.*

Applying Analytical Methods to Decision-making

Operations Research dates back to World War II, when military planners looked for ways to bring scientific calculations to Allied warfare. Operations Research can be defined as the discipline of applying advanced analytical methods to help make better decisions. By using techniques such as mathematical modeling, operations research give executives the power to make more effective decisions and build more productive systems. Some typical methods and techniques used in operations research include:

1. Simulation – gives one the ability to try out approaches and test ideas.
2. Optimization – narrows choices down to the very best and compares them.
3. Probability and statistics – helps to measure risk, mines data to find valuable connections and insights, tests conclusions, and makes reliable forecasts.
4. Mathematical models.
5. Algorithms (complex).
6. Visualization.
7. Neural networks.
8. Pattern recognition.
9. Data mining and data warehousing.

Operations Research supports an indefinite number of business decisions, including capital budgeting, asset allocation, portfolio selection, fraud prevention, benchmarking, customer segmentation, direct marketing campaigns, supply chain planning, distribution, resource allocation, inventory planning, product mix and blending, and industrial waste reduction, to name a few.

Strategically Monitoring and Managing the Performance of a Company

Performance Management describes the methodologies, metrics, processes, systems and software that are used for monitoring and managing the business performance of an enterprise.

Primary benefits of PM:
1. *Serves to maximize value creation consistently.*
2. *Helps to increase corporate transparency.*
3. *Facilitates communication with investors, analysts, and stakeholders.*
4. *Improves internal communication on strategy.*
5. *Facilitates the improvement of decision making.*
6. *Helps balance short -term, middle-term, and long-term trade-offs.*
7. *Encourages value -creating investments.*
8. *Improves the allocation of resources; streamlines planning and budgeting.*
9. *Serves to better deal with increased complexity and greater uncertainty and risk.*

Using Indigenous Change Agents

According to Richard Tanner Pascale and Jerry Sternin, there are always positive exceptions to the rules. In some ways, a few isolated groups or individuals, while operating under the same rules as everyone else, are faring better. In the HBR of 2005, they describe their Positive Deviance method, which holds that managers must actively look for such groups or individuals and bring their success strategies into the mainstream.

Pascale and Sternin make the following comparison of the Traditional Approach to Change vs. the Positive Deviance Approach to Change:

Traditional Approach to Change	Positive Deviance Approach to Change
Leadership as Path Breaker	Leadership as Inquiry
Outside-in	Inside-out
Deficit-based	Asset-based
Logic-driven	Learning-driven
Vulnerable to Transplant Rejection	Open to Self-Replication
Flows from Problem Solving towards Solution Identification	Flows from Solution Identification towards Problem Solving
Focused on the Protagonists	Focused on Enlarging the Network

Figure 5.1

There are six steps involved in the process of Positive Deviance:

1. *Make the group the guru* – Champions and Change Leaders are important, but often these individuals generate unconstructive dependence from their teams.
2. *Reframe through facts* – problems must be restated.
3. *Make it safe to learn* – a safe environment must be created that supports innovative ideas.
4. *Make the problem concrete.*
5. *Leverage social proof* – find examples of solutions that have worked in similar situations.
6. *Confound the immune defense response* – prevent

avoidance, resistance, and exceptionalism; let the change feel natural.

The Positive Deviance method works best in situations where behavioral and attitude changes are needed and there is no off-the-shelf remedy. It facilitates a role reversal where teachers become students and leaders become followers.

It is not suited for change initiatives around proven remedies to technical problems or for problems that rely on brainpower but that don't require major behavioral adjustments. Additionally, it may not be simple to create a safe environment for the birth of innovative ideas.

Understanding Value Creation along 5 Focus Areas

The Skandia Navigator is a collection of intangibles measurements methods, pioneered by Leif Edvinsson. Five focus areas capture different areas of interest. The Skandia Navigator facilitates a holistic understanding of the organization and its value creation along 5 focus areas (See figure 5.2 on the next page).

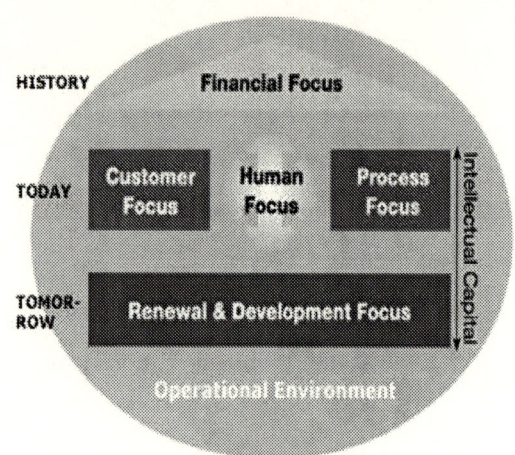

Figure 5.2

1. *Financial focus captures the financial outcome of activities. It is here where businesses establish long-term goals as well as a large part of the overall conditions for the other perspectives.*
2. *Customer focus gives an indication of how well the organization meets the needs of its customers via services and products. How loyal are the organization's customers?*
3. *Process focus captures the actual processes of creating the services and products that customers want. For example, how is customer support handled? It is also connected to internal processes.*
4. *Renewal and development focus aims at reassuring the organization's long-term renewal and, in part, its sustainability. What steps should be taken now to ensure long-term growth?*
5. *Human focus is the heart of the organization. Satisfied employees lead to satisfied customers.*

Systematically Trying to Anticipate and Manage External Events and Trends of Strategic Significance

Strategic Risk Management is a technique used to devise and deploy a systematic approach for managing strategic risk, the array of external events and trends that can devastate a company's growth trajectory and shareholder value, as described by Adrian J. Slywotzky and John Drzik in the Harvard Business Review of April, 2005. Slywotzky and Drzik distinguish seven classes of strategic risk, with subcategories (typical countermeasures are in italics):

1. Industry
    - *Margin squeeze – shift the compete/collaboration ratio*
    - *Rising R&D/capital expenditure costs*
    - *Overcapacity*
    - *Commoditization*
    - *Deregulation*
    - *Increased power among suppliers*
    - *Extreme business-cycle volatility*
2. Technology
    - *Shift in technology – double bet*
    - *Patent expiration*
    - *Process becomes obsolete*
3. Brand
    - *Erosion – redefine scope of brand investment, reallocate brand investment*
    - *Collapse*
4. Competitor
    - *Emerging global rivals*

- Gradual market-share gainer
- One-of-a-kind competitor – create a new, non-overlapping business design

5. Customer
    - Customer priority shift – create and analyze proprietary information, conduct quick and cheap market experiments
    - Increasing customer power
    - Over-reliance on a few customers
6. Project – smart sequencing, developing excess options, employing the stepping-stone method
    - R&D failure
    - IT failure
    - Business development failure
    - Merger or acquisition failure
7. Stagnation
    - Flat or declining volume – generate "demand innovation"
    - Volume up, price down
    - Weak pipeline

It should be noted that certain financial, operational, and hazardous risks can potentially be of strategic significance, as well. The following steps comprise the strategic risk management process: identify and assess risks, map risks, quantify risks, identify potential positive consequences of risks, develop risk mitigation action plans, and adjust capital decisions.

Strategic Risk Management helps an organization to prepare for major risks, which may give it an edge over competitors. It can turn strategic threats into opportunities for growth, as well as assist an organization to better utilize capital. However, it must be kept in mind that no company can anticipate all risks.

Analyzing Personal and Organizational Thinking Preferences

In 1976, Ned Herrmann researched the brain as the source of creativity. The result of this research is the Herrmann Whole Brain Model.

Whole Brain Model

The Whole Brain Model can be used to analyze personal and organizational thinking preferences. Thinking preferences describe what we prefer, or not prefer, to pay attention to. Once an individual understands his or her thinking style, the door is open to improved communication, leadership, management, problem solving, decision making and other aspects of personal and interpersonal development. The four thinking styles illustrated in the Whole Brain Model are:

1. *Logician – Analytical, mathematical, technical, problem solving.*
2. *Organizer – Controlled, conservative, planned, organized.*
3. *Communicator – Interpersonal, emotional, musical, spiritual.*
4. *Visionary – Imaginative, artistic, holistic, synthesizing, conceptual.*

The Whole Brain Model supersedes "left brain/right brain" thinking in earlier models. According to Herrmann, dominant thinking in one of the four thinking styles causes the development of thinking preferences. Then these preferences establish our interests; foster the development of competencies, and influence our career choices and ultimately our work .

To Assess Management Systems and to Identify Major Improvement Areas

The Baldrige Award, established by Congress in 1987, assesses management systems, identifies major improvement areas, and aims to promote quality awareness. It is based on a weighted score of seven categories of performance criteria, the maximum attainable score being 1000: (See Figure 5.3 on the next page)

1 Leadership (120 pts.)
   1.1 Organizational Leadership (70 pts.)
   1.2 Social Responsibility (50 pts.)
2 Strategic Planning (85 pts.)
   2.1 Strategy Development (40 pts.)
   2.2 Strategy Deployment (45 pts.)
3 Customer and Market Focus (85 pts.)
   3.1 Customer and Market Knowledge (40 pts.)
   3.2 Customer Relationships and Satisfaction (45 pts.)

5 Human Resource Focus (85 pts.)
   5.1 Work Systems (35 pts.)
   5.2 Employee Learning and Motivation (25 pts.)
   5.3 Employee Well-Being and Satisfaction (25 pts.)
6 Process Management (85 pts.)
   6.1 Value Creation Processes (50 pts.)
   6.2 Support Processes (35 pts.)
7 Business Results (450 pts.)
   7.1 Customer-Focused Results (75 pts.)
   7.2 Product and Service

4 Measurement, Analysis, Knowledge Management (90 pts.)	Results (75 pts.)
4.1 Measurement and Analysis of Organizational Performance (45 pts.)	7.3 Financial and Market Results (75 pts.)
	7.4 Human Resource Results (75 pts.)
4.2 Information and Knowledge Management (45 pts.)	7.5 Organizational Effectiveness Results (75 pts.)
	7.6 Governance and Social Responsibility Results (75 pts.)

Figure 5.3

This model fits well in organizations taking a continuous improvement philosophy. It is aimed toward those organizations that are ethical, high-performing, and with high integrity. The 2005 Criteria have been updated to deal with specific pressures on senior leaders, the need for organizational, along with technological, innovation, and the challenges of long-term viability and sustainability.

The Role of the Corporate Centre in Strategy

The Parenting Styles theory of Michael Goold and Andrew Campbell focuses on the role of the corporate centre in a corporation. It argues that there are many approaches to corporate strategy based on management styles, but the planning Influence and the type of control influence by the centre are the two main determinants. From these, three generic stereotypes that companies tend to follow are identified: Financial Control, Strategic Planning, and Strategic Control.

The best type of influence or style to maximize value creation depends largely upon the corporate purpose, history and culture, and upon the reconciliation of multiple paradoxes of parenting advantage (control vs. empowerment, responsiveness vs. synergy, and portfolio vs. core competence).

Gradual, Continuous (incremental) Change (improvement)

The Kaizen method is a Japanese management concept of continuous incremental improvements. Key elements are: quality, effort, employee involvement, willingness to change, and communication. Kaizen is based on five elements: teamwork, personal discipline, improved morale, quality circles, and suggestions for improvements. Of these five, three key factors arise:

1. *Elimination of waste and inefficiency*
2. *The Kaizen five-S framework for good housekeeping a.*
    a. *Seiri – tidiness*
    b. *Seiton – orderliness*
    c. *Seiso – cleanliness*
    d. *Seiketsu – standardized clean -up*
    e. *Shitsuke – discipline*
3. *Standardization*

The Kaizen philosophy fits well in gradual, incremental change situations that require long -term change and in collective cultures. It is more people-oriented, easier to implement, but requires long-term discipline and provides only a small pace of change, compared to the Business Process Engineering method, which is technology-oriented and enables radical change but requires considerable change management skills.

Finding the Root Cause of a problem (Root Cause Analysis)

This is a structured technique step by step technique that focuses on finding the real cause of a problem and dealing with that. It ascertains and analyzes the cause of problems.

Usage of Root Cause Analysis Benefits:

Most problems that arise in corporations have multiple approaches to deal with them. The optimum is to find the solution that most quickly deals with the situation. Usually the symptoms are treated rather than finding the underlying fundamental problem that is the root cause. The goal of a Root Cause Analysis is to find out:

1. *What happened*

2. *Why it happened*

3. *What can be done to prevent the problem from happening again.*

Because of physical conditions, human behavior,

behavior of systems, etc., several causes will usually be found for any given problem. Here's how the root cause analysis process works. First one asks why the situation occurred. Then the answers are recorded. And then it i s necessary to ask why for each answer again and again. Contributing factors are identified. Then we find the best method to change the root cause so we can improve our current condition. That is a process commonly known as corrective and preventive actions.

Brainstorming

This is a semi structured creative group activity used most often in ad-hoc business meetings to come up with new ideas for innovation or improvement. Members of the group are encouraged to put forward ideas about a problem and how it may be solved in order to generate as many ideas as possible even if they are not always feasible. The idea is that a group of people can achieve a higher (synergy) level of creativity than the sum of the participants separately.

Guidelines:

1. *Participants should be encouraged to come up with as many ideas as possible (and none are to be considered "bad").*
2. *No judgment rendered until the end of the session.*
3. *Build on each other's ideas creating unlikely combinations, taking each in unexpected directions.*

The following tips will help in almost any brainstorming session:
- o *Use an experienced facilitator.*
- o *Appoint one person to note down ideas that*

          come forth.
- *Use a flip chart for the notes.*
- *Identify precise topics for discussion.*
- *No more than 8 to 10 people per group.*
- *Evaluate the ideas in 2 steps.*
  - *define the criteria.*
  - *score the results.*
- *Welcome creativity.*
- *Encourage everyone to participate.*
- *Let people have fun with it.*

Business Intelligence

This refers to the practice of making better business decisions through the use of timely and accurate information. One uses a broad category of Management Information Systems, applications and technologies for gathering, storing, analyzing and providing access to data.

Typical BI activities would include support and query reporting, online analytical processing, statistical analysis, forecasting and data mining. BI represent those systems that help companies understand what makes the corporation successful and to help predict the future impact of current decisions.

Application for BI could include profiling, market basket analysis, anti-money laundering, anti-fraud, customer contact analysis, market segmentation, credit scoring, and product profitability.

Forecasting

Forecasting is a means of estimating the future. While nobody can look into the future, modern statistical methods, economic models and business intelligence software can to some extent help businesses forecast and estimate what is going to happen in the future.

ARIMA stands for Auto Regressive Integrated Moving Average. It was first developed in the late 60's but was systemized by Box and Jenkins in 1976. ARIMA can be more complex to use than other statistical forecasting techniques, although when implemented properly ARIMA can be quite powerful and flexible. ARIMA determines two things:

1. How much of the past should be used to predict the next observation.
2. The value of the weights to be used.

In using ARIMA, care should be taken to identify and estimate parameters as outliers (pulses, level shifts, local time trends, etc).

Explanation of Gestalt Theory

The essence of successful problem solving, according to Wertheimer, is to be able to see the overall structure of the problem. Two directions are involved: getting a whole consistent picture and seeing what the structure of the whole requires for the parts.

According to Wolfgang Kohler, basically the theory holds "there are wholes which instead of being the sum of parts existing indecently, give their parts specific functions or properties that can only be defining in relation to the whole in question. The focus of GT is the idea of "grouping i.e. characteristics of stimuli cause us to structure or interpret a visual field or problem in a certain way.

Primary Factors of Grouping:

1. *Proximity. Elements tend to be grouped together.*
2. *Similarity. Items similar in some respect tend to be grouped together.*
3. *Closure. Items are grouped together if they tend to complete some entity.*
4. *Simplicity. Items will be organized into simple figures according to symmetry, regularity and smoothness.*

These factors are called the laws of organization and are explained in the context of perception and problem solving. Human beings are viewed as open systems in active interaction with their environment. There are wholes, the behavior of which is not determined by that of their individual element but where the part processes are themselves determined by the intrinsic nature of the whole. The theory is not limited only to the concept of the Gestalt or the whole but must be seen far broader and more encompassing.

1. *Primacy of the phenomenal. Recognizing and taking seriously the human world of experience as the only immediately given reality.*
2. *It is the interaction of the individual and the situation in the sense of a dynamic field that determines experience and behavior, and not only drive (psychoanalyst*

ethnology) or external stimuli (behaviorism), or static personality traits (classical personality theory).

3. *Connections among psychological contents are more readily and more permanently created on the basis of substantive concrete relationships than by sheer repetition and reinforcement.*
4. *Thinking and problem solving are characterized by appropriate substantive organization, restructuring and centering of the given (insight) in the direction of the desired solution.*
5. *In memory, structures based on associative connections are elaborated and differentiated according to a tendency for optimal organization*
6. *Cognitions which an individual cannot integrate, lead to an experience of dissonance. And toward cognitive processes directed at reducing this dissonance*
7. *In a supra individual whole such as a group, there is a tendency towards specific relationships in the interaction of strengths and needs.*

Large Scale Statistical Forecasting

The Exponential Smoothing Model is another method of helping companies to make forecasts. It does this by using a weighted average of past and current values, adjusting weight on current values to account for the effects of swings in the data, such as seasonality. The sensitivity of the smoothing effects can be adjusted by using an alpha term (between 0 and 1). ESM gives more weight to recent observations. There are one or more smoothing parameters that must be determined. These choices establish the weights assigned to the observations.

Analyze the Rate at which Innovations are Adopted

The Rogers Innovation Adoption Curve is a model that classifies adopters of innovations into various categories, and is based on the idea that some are more open for adaptation than others. Research focuses on:

1. *Characteristics of an innovation that may influence its adoption*
2. *Decision-making process to adopt a new idea or product*
3. *An individual's characteristics that make them likely to adopt an innovation*
4. *Consequences for both individuals and society of adopting an innovation*
5. *Communication channels used in the adoption process*

Curve categories:

1. *Innovators: brave people, pulling the change*
2. *Early adopters: respectable people, opinion leaders, try new ideas carefully*
3. *Early majority: thoughtful people, accept change quicker than average people*
4. *Late majority: skeptical people, will use new products only when majority does*
5. *Laggards: traditional people, stick to "old ways", critical about new ideas and will accept them only when idea has become mainstream or even tradition*

The Adoption Curve shows that it is better to first convince the innovators and the early adopters instead of trying to convince the mass.

Decision Making with Risks that Cannot be Known

The Plausibility Theory provides new insights into decision making with risks that cannot be known. Before the Plausibility theory, the common theory used by scientists was Bayesian statistics. According to Bayesian theory, managers should make decisions based on a calculation of the probabilities of all the possible outcomes of a situation. At first look, this method seems workable. However, this method faces at least two phenomena that are difficult to explain: the appreciation of downside risk, and how to deal with risks that can't be known.

Both of these phenomena can be dealt with when the "expected value" of a Bayesian calculation is replaced with the "risk threshold" of the Plausibility Theory. As with its predecessor, the Plausibility Theory assesses the range of outcomes, but focuses on the probability of hitting a threshold point, such as a net loss, relative to an acceptable risk. For example, a normally profitable decision is rejected if there is a higher than 2% risk of making a major loss.

Chapter 6 - Program and Project Management

"It must be considered that there is nothing more difficult to carry out nor more doubtful of success nor more dangerous to handle than to initiate a new order of things" - Machiavelli 1446 -1507, Italian statesman and philosopher

Result Oriented Management

This is a management style described by Jan Schouten and Wim van Beers. The aim is to achieve maximum results based on clear and measurable agreements made previously. The theory postulates that people will work with more enthusiasm if they:

1. *clearly know what is expected of them.*
2. *are involved in establishing the expectations.*
3. *are allowed to determine for themselves how they are going to meet these expectations.*

The Experience Curve Effect

First propounded by Bruce Henderson in 1960, this idea demonstrates that there is a consistent relationship between the cost of production and the cumulative production quantity. As tasks are performed more often, the cost of performing the tasks will decrease. When the cumulative volume doubles, the value added costs will fall by a constant and predictable percentage. The observed experience curve ranges from between 10 and 30 percent.

The Experience Curve is a major enabler for a cost leadership strategy. If a company can gain a big market share quickly in a new market, it has a competitive cost advantage because it can produce products cheaper than its competitors. Thus, if a company could accelerate its production experience by increasing its market share it could gain a cost advantage in its industry that would be hard to equal.

Five Evolutionary Stages in Managing Organizational Processes

The Capability Maturity Model (CMM) describes the principles and practices underlying software process maturity. The focus is on identifying key process areas and the exemplary practices that may comprise a disciplined software process. The maturity framework provided by CMM establishes a context in which practices can be repeated, best practices can be quickly transferred across groups, thus providing some standardization, variations in performing best practices are reduced, and practices are being continuously improved to enhance capability. There are five stages in the CMM:

1. *Initial (processes are chaotic, or not defined at all).*
2. *Repeatable (basic processes are established).*
3. *Defined (all processes defined, documented, standardized, and integrated into each other).*
4. *Managed (processes are measured by collecting detailed data on the process quality).*
5. *Optimizing (continuous process improvement is adopted and in place by quantitative feedback).*

The Capability Maturity Model is structured in this way:

1. *Maturity Levels – layered framework that provides a progression to the discipline. It is important to note that an organization develops the ability to assess the impact of a new practice, technology, or tool on their ability. Hence, it is not a matter of adopting these, but it is a matter of determining how innovative efforts influence existing practices.*
2. *Key Process Areas – identify clusters of related activities that, when performed collectively, achieve a set of goals considered important.*
3. *Goals – summarize the states that must exist for that key process area. Their success indicates how much capability the organization has established at that maturity level.*
4. *Common Features – include practices that implement and institutionalize a key process area.*
5. *Key Practices – describe the elements of infrastructure and practice that contribute most effectively to the implementation of the key process areas.*

The Process Definition Criteria is established by asking the question, "What software process information do I need to document?" It must be included in a software process description for it to be usable by those performing the process. These process elements are: purpose, input, output, role, activity, entry criteria, exit criteria, procedure, reviews and audits, work products, measurements, training, and tools.

Measuring the Effectiveness of Program Management

Earned Value Management is an integrated program measurement and management technique that relates resource planning to schedules, technical cost and schedule requirements. The two major objectives of EVM are:

1. *To encourage contractors to use effective internal cost and schedule systems.*
2. *To permit customers to be able to rely on timely data produced by those systems to determine product - oriented contract status.*

This data allows EVM to project future performance based on trends to date and allows better and more effective management decision making to minimize adverse impacts to the project. Using the EVM process, management can readily compare how much work has actually been completed against the amount of work the company is planning to accomplish.

Managing the Tension between (Value) Creation and Control

In 1995, Robert Simons introduced the Levers of Control framework, giving managers in large companies a framework to manage the tension between creation (value) and control (managing and measuring value). Levers of Control are formal information-based routines or procedures that are used by management to maintain or alter patterns in organizational behavior. Simons has identified five Levers of Control:

1. *Internal Controls. Customary safeguards that a company establishes to protect assets and ensure reliable record-keeping.*
2. *Belief Systems. An organization must put such systems in place to control commitment to the organization's vision, core values, mission statements, credos and statements of purpose.*
3. *Boundary Systems. Must-haves for organizations to stake out the territory for each participant: codes of conduct, operational guidelines, etc.*
4. *Diagnostic Control Systems. Must be in place so a company can optimize outcomes and get the work done.*
5. *Interactive Control Systems. For tracking new ideas, triggering new learning, and properly positioning the organization for the future: incorporating process data into management interaction, face-to-face meetings with employees, challenging data, assumptions and action plans of subordinates.*

Simons recommends the following questions to understand an organization better:

1. *Have senior managers communicated core values so people understand and embrace?*
2. *Have managers clearly identified forbidden actions and behaviors?*
3. *Are diagnostic control systems adequately monitoring critical performance variables?*
4. *Are control systems interactive, and designed to stimulate learning?*
5. *Are you paying enough for traditional internal controls?*

The answers to these questions can be key components of change once they have been thoroughly reviewed and analyzed.

Managing Successful Programs

The Managing Successful Programs (MSP) method, developed by the Office of Government Commerce (OGC), an independent office of the U K Treasury, is a program management framework for benefits identification and delivery. It deals with achieving the Vision Statement, which describes to the organization's internal and external customers the definition of what to expect from the organization in the future. MSP includes a document known as "The Blueprint" that sets out the structure and composition of the changed organization that, after delivery, should demonstrate the capabilities in the Vision Statement. There are six steps in the MSP method:

1. *Identifying a Program. To sponsor the program, confirm the program mandate, appoint the senior responsible owner, produce the program brief, and develop terms of reference for program definition, review, and approve to proceed.*
2. *Defining a Program. To establish the team to define the program, to develop the vision statement, blueprint, and benefit profiles, to validate the benefits, identify stakeholders, design the project portfolio, identify tranches (where projects and activities are grouped), design organization structure, develop the business case and governance arrangements, develop the communications plan, the benefits realization plan, the program plan, and to approve to proceed.*
3. *Governing a Program. To set up the program organization and office, to support governance requirements, to set up the physical program environment, risk management and issue resolution, HR management, procurement and contract management, program communications, reporting -monitoring-control, information management, reviews, and to maintain business as usual.*
4. *Managing the Portfolio. Project startup, to align projects with benefits realization and program objectives, to monitor progress, manage risks and resolve issues, project closure, and manage stakeholders.*

5. *Managing Benefits. To establish benefits measurement, refine benefits profiles, monitor benefits, manage transition, support changes to culture and personnel, support benefit realization, and measure benefits.*
6. *Closing a Program. To confirm program closure, program review, update and finalize program information, to disband program management team and support function, and to inform stakeholders.*

Some benefits to this method are:

1. *More effective delivery of changes since they can be implemented in an integrated way.*
2. *Alignment between the strategy and project levels.*
3. *Management support.*
4. *More effective resource management.*
5. *Better risk management.*
6. *Benefits realization.*
7. *Budgetary control.*
8. *Improved performance.*
9. *More effective management of the business case.*
10. *More efficient coordination & control.*
11. *Smooth transition management.*
12. *Consistency.*

MSP does not provide a prescriptive process and does not include all ingredients. For example, it notes that you need a refined business case, but does not explain how to create it. It only discusses one program although there may be many programs interrelated to each other. In order for MSP to work, suitable resources must be available and senior management has to agree with the change and actively sponsor it.

Managing Projects, Programs and Portfolios to Achieve its Strategic Goals

Organizational Project Management Maturity Model, or OPM3, which helps organizations to assess their level of maturity by analyzing best practices, was developed by the Project Management Institute (PMI). There are three domains in OPM3: projects, programs and portfolios. After gaining knowledge of what constitutes best practices, an assessment can be performed of the organization's current maturity level. Then a directory of best practices and defined capabilities is used to define a path for improvement.

OPM3 is a scalable and generic model, and can be applied to profit and nonprofit organizations of different sizes, industries and geographical locations. It is the first model to describe best practices for project, program and portfolio management, and focuses on the clear correlation between an organization's abilities to manage such and its effectiveness in implementing strategy.

Transferring Business Processes

Outsourcing is a strategic management model where business processes are transferred to another company in order to let a third party service provider perform the management and/or daily execution of one or more business functions. The aim is mostly to make an organization more competitive by staying focused on its core competencies.

There are many benefits of outsourcing: renewed focus on core business, mitigation of risks, project and service improvements, skills upgrade, retention, and access, technology infusion, cost reduction, asset conversion, and avoidance of capital investment, to name a few. There are various terms that are associated with Outsourcing:

1. *Application Service Provider (ASP) : a company that provides applications and related services over the Internet. (Includes e-mail, payroll processing and ERP applications).*

2. *Business Process Outsourcing (BPO) : outsourcing of Back Office and Front Office functions. (Includes accounting, HR, and medical coding and transcription).*

3. *Competitive Insourcing : a process where internal employees are competing in bidding against competitive, third-party bidders for a defined scope of work.*

4. *Contract Manufacturing: the outsourcing of a manufacturing job to an onshore or offshore third -party.*

5. *Co-sourcing: where a business function is performed by both internal staff and external resources, such as consultants or outsourcing vendors.*

6. *Facilities Management: an outsourcing solution in which the customer entrusts the responsibility*

for operations and maintenance of one or more facilities to an external provider.

7. *Insourcing: the transfer of an outsourced function to an internal department of a company to be managed entirely by employees.*

8. *Nearshoring: outsourcing within nearby territory, accessible by short travel or telephone in the same or neighboring time zone.*

9. *Offshoring: outsourcing overseas or in a separate country.*

10. *Service Level Agreement (SLA): a contract or contract addendum that defines the type, value and conditions of the outsourcing services to be provided.*

11. *Shared Services: the outsourcing of a business function within an enterprise to a highly skilled internal department or group.*

Project Management Methodology

Originally developed in 1989 by the Central Computer and Telecommunications Agency (CCTA), PRINCE2 (PRojects IN Controlled Environments) focuses on organization, management and control. It is process-based, each process being defined with key inputs and outputs, objectives to be achieved, and activities to be carried out. It is also product-based, meaning the project plans are focused on delivering results, and is driven by the project's business case that describes the justification, commitment and rationale for the outcome. PRINCE2 can be used for both IT and non-IT projects. See figure 6.1 below.

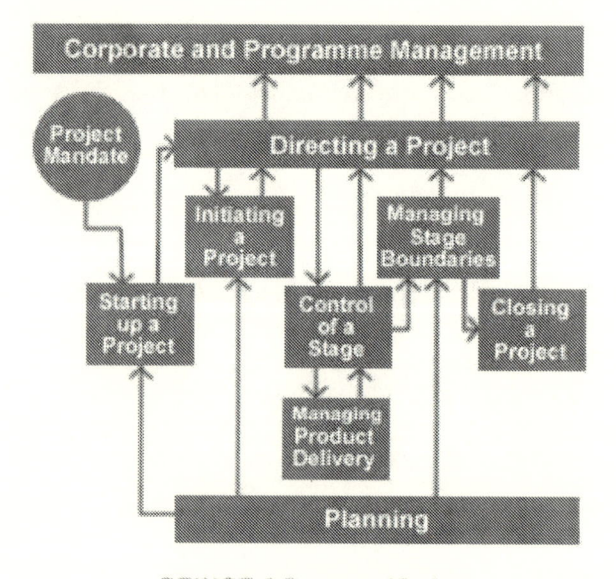

PRINCE 2 Process Model

Figure 6.1

There are 8 steps in the PRINCE2 framework:

1. *Directing a Project. Project Board members should ensure that support is provided without excessive time commitment.*
2. *Starting up a Project. Initial ideas are qualified and a Project Board, representing user, supplier and business interests, is appointed.*
3. *Initiating a Project. Qualifying a project to ensure it is*

likely to meet its objectives, and guaranteeing organizational buy-in before major resources are committed.
4. *Controlling a Stage. A Project Manager's daily steps taken to manage work, react to events and escalate major issues.*
5. *Managing Product Delivery. The steps teams should take to agree on work packages, report on progress, and deliver completed work.*
6. *Managing Stage Boundaries. Project Board review preparation when progress and future plans are discussed, and out of tolerance conditions are handled.*
7. *Closure. Closing down a project, handling follow-up on actions, and handling post project benefit reviews.*
8. *Planning. Regardless of when the planning is done.*

PRINCE2 embodies proven and established good practices in the management of projects. Since it is a widely recognized method, it provides a common language. It allows projects to have an organized start, middle and end, regular progress reviews, and encourages communication. Individual projects benefit through definition of roles and responsibilities at each level, reduced meetings, appropriate levels of planning, and ways of managing changes. PRINCE2 does not, however, cover contract management or people management.

Entrepreneurial Government

According to David Osborne and Ted Gaebler, governments do not work well because they are tall, sluggish, over-centralized, and preoccupied with rules and regulations. They recommend Entrepreneurial Government, a government that can compete and, indeed, must compete with for-profit businesses, nonprofit agencies, and other units of government. Following is a list of ten principles of reinvention, as suggested by Osborne and Gaebler. The Entrepreneurial Government should be:

1. Catalytic: steering rather than rowing.
2. Community owned: empowering rather than serving.
3. Competitive: injecting competition into service delivery.
4. Mission-driven: transforming rule-driven organizations.
5. Results oriented: funding outcomes, not inputs.
6. Customer-driven: meeting the needs of the customer, not the bureaucracy.
7. Enterprising: earning rather than spending.
8. Anticipatory: prevention rather than cure.
9. Decentralized: from hierarchy towards participation and teamwork.
10. Market-oriented: leveraging change through the market.

Osborne and Gaebler's model for Entrepreneurial Government has led to the initiation of the National Performance Review (NPR) by Vice President Al Gore in 1994.

Developing and Delivering Near-Perfect Products and Services

The Six Sigma model, based on the statistical work of Joseph Juran and pioneered by Mikel Harry and Motorola, is a quality management methodology that provides businesses with the tools to improve the capability of their business processes and leads to defect reduction and improvement in profits, employee morale, and product quality. It focuses on the control of a process until the point of six sigma from a centerline, or 3.4 defects per million. The model's central idea is that if you can measure how many defects you have in a process, you can also figure out how to eliminate them. There are five stages in the Six Sigma process:

1. *Definition. Define what constitutes a defect, then establish a set of objectives designed to reduce the occurrence of such defects.*
2. *Measurement. Gather data and prepare it for high-level analysis.*
3. *Analysis. Identify ways in which people fail to ensure effective control at each stage.*
4. *Improvement. Recommend, decide and implement improvements.*
5. *Control. Create controls to enable the company to sustain and extend improvements.*

The Study and Management of Complex Feedback

Systems Thinking is an approach for studying and managing complex feedback systems. The term system means an interdependent group of things forming a unified pattern. Feedback refers to how X affects Y, and, conversely, how Y affects X. One cannot study X or Y independently.

System Dynamics, developed by Jay W. Forrester, is similar to System Thinking, but includes constructing and testing a computer simulation model. The following are the steps in the System Dynamics methodology:

1. *Identify a problem.*
2. *Develop a hypothesis explaining the cause of such problem.*
3. *Build a computer simulation model of the system at the root of the problem.*
4. *Test the model to confirm that it faithfully reproduces real world behavior.*
5. *Devise and test alternative policies that may alleviate the problem.*
6. *Implement the solution.*

System Dynamics can be applied in many situations, such as strategy and corporate planning, business process development, public management and policy, biological and medical modeling, energy and the environment, and dynamic decision making, to name a few.

Identifying and Decreasing Waste

The Value Stream Mapping method, pioneered by Toyota's chief engineer, Taiichi Ohno, and sensei Shigeo Shingo, is a visualization tool oriented to the Toyota version of Lean Manufacturing. Its goal is to identify, demonstrate and decrease waste in the process. VSM is a starting point, then, to help recognize waste and identify its causes. Therefore, it is primarily a communication tool, but can also be used as a strategic planning tool and a change management tool.

The Value Stream Mapping method visually maps the flow of materials and information from the moment products enter the back door as raw materials to the moment they leave the loading dock as finished products. Mapping out these activities with cycle times, down times, in-process inventory, material moves, and information flows helps to visualize the process activities and guides toward the future desired state. There are seven original commonly accepted wastes in the Toyota production system (with reformulation between brackets by Jones, 1995):

1. *Overproduction (faster than necessary pace).*
2. *Waiting.*
3. *Transport (conveyance).*
4. *Inappropriate processing*
5. *Unnecessary inventory (excess inventory).*
6. *Unnecessary motion.*
7. *Defects (correction of mistakes).*

Peter Hines and Nick Rich, from their article published in International Journal of Operations & Production Management, 1997, have suggested the following tools:

1. *Process activity mapping*
2. *Supply chain response matrix*
3. *Production variety funnel*
4. *Quality filter mapping*
5. *Demand amplification mapping*
6. *Decision point analysis*

7. *Physical structure mapping*

Comparing Programs with Each Other

The Programme Management Maturity Model (PMMM), developed by ProgM, the joint program management special interest group of the British Computer Society and the Association for Project Management, provides a mechanism through which an organization can make an assessment of itself.

There are 10 key program management processes:

1. *Management organization.*
2. *Program planning.*
3. *Management of benefits.*
4. *Management of stakeholders.*
5. *Issue management & risk management.*
6. *Quality management & auditing.*
7. *Configuration management.*
8. *Internal communication.*
9. *Accounts and finances.*
10. *Management of scope & change.*

Each stage of maturity for each process is summarized by a question. A program is then rated based on the answers to these questions. The ratings are converted into a visual profile that shows which of the selected 10 aspects of program development are well developed and which are not.

To utilize this process, an organization must complete the self-assessment via a questionnaire and send the questionnaire to ProgM. Then the organization will receive a profile.

This program allows organizations to benchmark themselves against similar organizations, the programs may be compared with each other, and there is presently no cost to using this model. However, self-assessment must be honest or the model will not be useful.

Chapter 7 - Organizational Change and Transformation

"Social organizations are flagrantly open systems in that the input of energies and the conversion of output into further energetic input consists of transactions between the organization and its environment" - Daniel Katz and Robert L. Kahn in The Social Psychology of Organizations (1966)

The 7 S Framework

The organizational structure of any company is comprised of a number of separate yet interdependent factors. These have been categorized by McKinsey into seven key components known as the 7 S Framework. The model was first mentioned in "The Art of Japanese Management" in 1981.

At the center of this framework is the concept of Shared Values. Every company has something to which it owes its identity. What does the company stand for? What is its purpose? The other parts of the framework are built on this centerpiece. Strategy is self-explanatory. This emphasizes the importance of some sort of strategic blueprint for the company that will clearly define how it plans to meet its objectives. Structure explains how the company is organized. Is it centralized? Decentralized? Broken into numerous divisions? Whichever the case may be, structure will effect every aspect of how the company does business.

System describes the procedures that a company has in place to conduct day-to-day operations. No company can operate effectively without a well thought out, systematic way of doing things.

Staff is of course the company's workforce, which is responsible for both managing the company and carrying out its assignments. Style is another way of defining the company's corporate culture. There is a distinct atmosphere, a way of doing and understanding things, which is at least come degree unique to each individual company. This not only builds a team atmosphere, but it helps to establish corporate identity. The final S is Skill. This is the cumulative weight of the company's talents, which helps to give it an edge in the workplace.

The 7 S model is an organizational tool that helps to keep companies focused on the their particular place within the "big picture" of the overall industry.

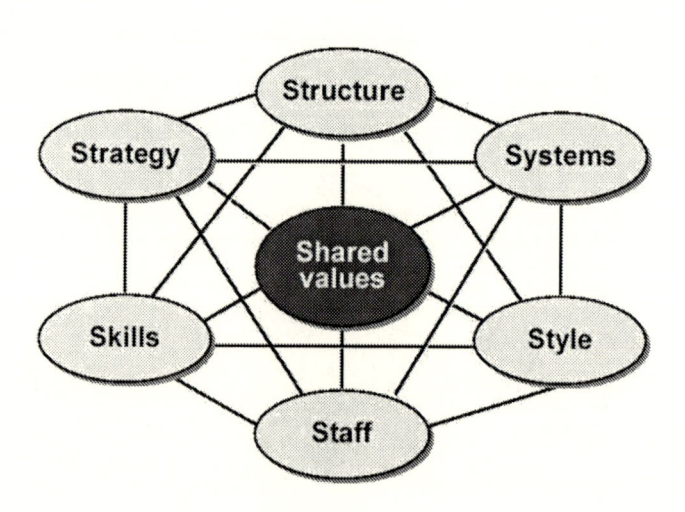

Figure 7.1

The Three C's

Several renowned business strategy gurus adhere to the business model that stresses a three-pronged approach to strategy called the three C's: These are the corporation itself, the customer, and the competition.

The first is a corporate based strategy that aims at maximizing the corporation's competitive position in the industry. Suggested methods include selectivity and sequencing. The idea here is that the corporation need only gain a decisive position in one key function and by so doing will be able to improve its other functions, which may be mediocre. An example would be that in a time of rapid wage increases perhaps it is time to make a decision about subcontracting out the expensive part of the assembly operation. This can result in a significant competitive advantage.

Another suggestion is cost cutting by either exerciseing greater selectivity in terms of orders accepted, products offered or maybe something as radical as sharing a key function with another of the corporation's businesses or even with other companies.

The second part of the triad may seem obvious in that a company's first concern ought to be the interests of its customers rather than the stockholders. But paradoxical as that might seem, if the customer is taken care of then ultimately the stockholder will be too. They are not exclusive interests. Consider this example. People drink coffee for different reasons. Therefore the market has several segments (the various kinds of coffee drinkers). A marketing cost survey measured against market coverage may show that there could be a point of diminishing returns in this relationship. So it is now clear that the company must optimize its market coverage so that its cost will be competitive.

If it is found that even more segmenting is necessary because of competition it may be necessary to re-examine the customer base and further define its needs. If it is found that market forces are changing the customer mix, then this means that the company must allocate or shift its resources.

Finally, there is the customer based strategy. To devise this strategy the company must look at possible sources of differentiation with its competitors in functions such as purchasing, design, engineering, sales and servicing. For example, if it is difficult to find a difference between your product and the competitors' products, you may be left with only advertising or PR to maintain an edge.

It is suggested that a company can exploit source of profit, for example from sales to service. New car dealers, for instance, make more from service add-ons than from the sale itself. In a sluggish market the company with fixed cost ratios can lower prices to win more market share to the detriment of companies with high fixed costs.

There is a benefit for smaller companies that can't afford to compete in advertising or massive R and D efforts. The small company can calculate its incentives on a gradual percentage basis, thus guaranteeing their distributors larger profits per unit. This is effective against big marketers.

Japanese strategists believe that streamlined corporate management can be achieved when corporate assets of people, money and things are competently expended. For example, cash left over from what is needed is wasted. It is better to allocate funds last. Rather, people (talent) should come first based on the available plant and equipment. Thus when the people (talent) have created ideas and strategies, then the money would be more wisely allocated.

Business Modeling through Simulation

This refers to identifying the right area to change and improve the overall success of an organization. Tools are needed to help managers truly understand their business processes and how modifications to those processes will impact the company.

It is the technique to model business processes. Business models provide ways of expressing business processes or strategies in terms of business activities and collaborative behavior so we can better understand the business process and the participants in the process.

With the aid of this software managers can understand their business processes like never before It can show the flow of work through a system using graphs, showing problem areas. The system can be used to correct the problem. It also allows non technical personnel to try out various options or scenarios to assist in the decision making. Simulation serves the following uses:

1. *Financial planning*
2. *Risk Management*
3. *Forecasting*
4. *Business process Modeling*

145

The Theory of Mechanistic and Organic Systems

Developed by Burns and Stalker, this is a way to understand which organization forms fit to specific circumstances of change or stability. They provide the following characteristics of Mechanistic vs. Organic Systems:

1. *Appropriate Conditions -- Stable vs. Changing.*

2. *Distribution of Tasks -- Specialized differentiation of fictional tasks facing a concern as a whole are broken down.*

3. *Nature of Individual task -- Here, the functionaries tend to pursue the technical improvements of means rather than the accomplishment of the ends of the concern.*

4. *Who defines tasks or refines tasks -- The reconciliation for each level in the hierarchy, of these distinct performances by the immediate superiors.*

5. *Task scope -- The precise definition of rights and methods attached to each functional role.*

6. *How is task conformance ensured -- The translation of obligations into the responsibilities of a functional position.*

The Change Management Iceberg

The Change Management Iceberg of Wilfried Kruger is a strong visualization of what is arguably the essence of change in organizations: dealing with barriers. Many change managers only consider the top of the iceberg; cost, quality and time.

Below the surface, however, there are two more dimensions and implementation management. They are management of perception and beliefs and power and politics management. The kind of change can be hard things (information systems) or soft things (values mindsets and capabilities) The applied change strategy involves revolutionary, dramatic changes or the evolutionary, incremental changes.

People involved in the change. Opponents have both a negative general attitude towards change and a negative behavior towards this particular personal change. Promoters have both a position generic attitude and are positive about this particular change.

Five Disciplines

In his book "The Fifth Discipline", Peter Senge wants to destroy the illusion that the world is created out of separate, unrelated forces. When we give up this illusion, we can then build 'learning organizations', where people continually expand their capacity to create the results they truly desire. The five components in the model from Senge are:

1. *Systems Thinking. The integrative (fifth) discipline that fuses the other 4 into a coherent body of theory and*

practice.
2. *Personal Mastery.* People must regard their life and their work such as an artist would regard a work of art.
3. *Mental Models.* Deeply ingrained assumptions or mental images that influence how we understand the world and how we take action.
4. *Building Shared Vision. If there is a genuine vision, people excel and learn, not because they have to, but because they want to.*
5. *Team Learning. Team-members participate in true dialogue. They suspend their assumptions.*

All of these five disciplines must be employed in a never-ending quest to expand the capacity of the organization to create its future.

Trajectories of Industry Change

Anita M. McGahan, Professor of Management in Boston published the model for The Four Trajectories of Industry Change in 2004. McGahan postulates that no organization can make intelligent investments without understanding how the particular industry is changing. She has developed four trajectories of industrial change:

1. *Radically. When core assets and core activities are both threatened with obsolescence.*
2. *Progressive. When neither core assets nor core activities are jeopardized.*

3. *Creative. When core assets are under threat but core activities are stable.*
4. *Intermediating. When core activities are threatened while core assets retain their capacity to create value.*

The Trajectories of Industry Change typically unfold themselves over decades. Fighting the industry change is almost always too costly to be worthwhile. Organizations should reconfigure themselves for lower revenue growth and look to their operations and materials use to find new ways to be profitable. Systematically analyzing the business environment is not easy, but the payoff is great.

Catastrophe Theory

Catastrophe Theory (CT), developed by René Thom, is a mathematical treatment of continuous action producing a discontinuous result. Although it was developed quite separately, it is now seen as a part of Chaos Theory.

Although of a highly mathematical nature, CT strives to explain change and discontinuity in systems. If a system is 'at rest' (i.e., not undergoing change), then it will tend to occupy a preferred stable state, or at least a defined range of states.

An analogy demonstrates the principle. Imagine that a bottle is placed on a desk. It is in a stable state, not changing, what is called Stable Equilibrium. Now imagine pushing the neck of the bottle away from you slowly with your finger, not too far. It is now undergoing change but the bottle is absorbing the change in a continuous manner. It is in

Unstable Equilibrium; if you release your pressure, the bottle will revert towards its stable and preferred position. However if you continue to push the neck of the bottle, at some point it will fall. It is now in a new stable equilibrium state. A Catastrophic Change has occurred. The method can be used to understand and to predict the behavior of complex systems. These would include:

1. Stock exchanges.
2. Locust infestations.
3. Biological change.
4. Behavior of bridges.
5. Attempts to apply Thom's theories to organizations so far had little real success, due to the large number of variables involved.

Changing Organization Cultures

In their excellent book "The Cultures of Work Organizations", Harrison Trice and Janice Beyer provide a number of ideas that you should remember and consider when you are changing the culture of an organization. The following considerations should be kept in mind when seeking to change an organization's culture:

1. *Capitalize on Propitious Moments. For example, poor financial performance. Make sure people actually perceive the need for change.*
2. *Combine Caution with Optimism. Create an optimistic outlook regarding what the change effort will bring.*
3. *Understand Resistance to Culture Change. Both at the*

individual level and at the organizational or group level.
4. *Change Many Elements, But Maintain Some Continuity. Identify the principles that will remain constant.*
5. *Recognize the Importance of Implementation. Initial acceptance and enthusiasm are insufficient to carry change forward:*
6. *Select, Modify, and Create Appropriate Cultural Forms. Employing symbols, rituals, languages, stories, myths, metaphors, rites, ceremonies.*
7. *Modify Socialization Tactics. If new socialization processes for new employees are instigated, an organization's culture will begin to change.*
8. *Find and Cultivate Innovative Leadership. Members are unlikely to give up whatever secure stability they derive from existing cultures and follow a leader in new directions unless that leader exudes self-confidence, has strong convictions, a dominant personality, and can preach the new vision with drama and eloquence.*

Competing Values Framework

Based on statistical analyses of a comprehensive list of effectiveness indicators, Quinn and Rohrbaugh (1983) discovered two major dimensions underlying conceptions of effectiveness.

The first dimension is related to organizational focus, from an internal emphasis on the well-being and development of people in the organization towards an external focus on the well-being and development of the organization itself.

The second dimension differentiates organizational

preference for structure and represents the contrast between stability and control and flexibility and change. Together the two dimensions form four quadrants.

The Competing Values Framework got its name because the criteria within the four models at first seem to carry conflicting messages. Organizations must be adaptable and flexible, but we want them at the same time to be stable and controlled.

The Competing Values Framework can be used in organizational context. It can be used as a strategic tool to develop supervision and management programs. It can also be used to help organizations diagnose their existing and desired cultures.

Quinn argues that more effective managers have the ability to play multiple, even competing leadership roles. Managers are expected to play all of these roles.

Defining Organizational Culture

With his Three Levels of Culture, Edgard Schein has provided an important contribution to defining what organizational culture actually is. Schein divides organizational culture into three levels:

> 1. *Artifacts. These "artifacts" are at the surface, those aspects (such as dress) that can be easily discerned, but are hard to understand.*
> 2. *Espoused Values. Beneath artifacts are "espoused values" which are conscious strategies, goals and philosophies.*

3. *Basic Assumptions and Values. The core, or essence, of culture is represented by the basic underlying assumptions and values, which are difficult to discern because they exist at a largely unconscious level. Yet they provide the key to understanding why things happen in a particular way.*

If managers do not become conscious of the cultures in which they are embedded, those cultures will manage them. Cultural understanding is desirable for everybody, but it is essential for leaders if they are to lead.

SWOT Analysis

A SWOT analysis is a tool used in management and strategy formulation. It can help to identify the Strengths, Weaknesses, Opportunities and Threats of a particular company.

The SWOT diagram is a very good tool for analyzing the (internal) strengths and weaknesses of a corporation and the (external) opportunities and threats. See Figure 7.2 on the next page.

Strengths	Weaknesses
• Specialist marketing expertise • Exclusive access to natural resources • Patents • New, innovative product or service • Location of your business • Cost advantage through proprietary know-how • Quality processes and procedures • Strong brand or reputation	• Lack of marketing expertise • Undifferentiated products and service (i.e. in relation to your competitors) • Location of your company • Competitors have superior access to distribution channels • Poor quality of goods or services • Damaged reputation
Opportunities	**Threats**
• Developing market (China, the Internet) • Mergers, joint ventures or strategic alliances • Moving into new attractive market segments • A new international market • Loosening of regulations • Removal of international trade barriers • A market that is led by a weak competitor	• A new competitor in your own home market • Price war • Competitor has a new, innovative substitute product or service • New regulations • Increased trade barriers • A potential new taxation on your product or service

Figure 7.2

Action Learning

Action Learning is a form of learning by doing. The process assembles a group of people with varied levels of skills and experience to analyze an actual work problem and develop an action plan. The ad-hoc group continues to meet as actions are implemented, learning from the implementation and making mid-course corrections.

Action learning programs involve small groups that meet regularly to take action on critical, real problems while explicitly seeking learning from having taken that action.

Dimensions of Change

In their book 'Managing Change for Competitive Success' (1991) Pettigrew and Whipp distinguish between three dimensions of strategic change.

1. *Content (objectives, purpose and goals) - WHAT*
2. *Process (implementation) - HOW*
3. *Context (the internal and external environment) - WHERE*

Pettigrew and Whipp emphasize the continuous interplay between these dimensions of change. The implementation of change is an iterative, cumulative and reformulation-in-use process. Successful change is a result of the interaction between the content (objectives, purpose and goals), the process (implementation) and the organizational context (the internal and external environment). The following are the five change factors identified by the authors:

1. *Environmental assessment. Continuous monitoring of both the internal and external environment [competition] of the organization through open learning systems.*
2. *Human resources as assets and liabilities. Employees should feel valued and they should know the organization trusts them.*
3. *Linking strategic and operational change. Bundling operational activities can lead to new strategic changes.*
4. *Leading the change. Move the organization ahead. Create the right climate for change. Coordinate activities. Set the agenda not only for the direction of the change, but also for the right vision and values.*
5. *Overall coherence. A change strategy should be consistent, consonant, provide a competitive edge and be feasible.*

Explanation of RACI, RASCI and RACIC

The acronym, RACI, is broken down in the following manner:

- R = Responsible. Person owns the problem / project.
- A = to whom "R" is Accountable. He or she must sign or approve the work before it is OK.
- S = Supportive. Can provide resources or can play a supporting role in implementation.
- C = Consulted. Holds information and/or capability necessary to complete the work.

- *I = Informed. Must be notified of results, but need not be consulted.*

The technique is typically supported by a RACI chart which helps to discuss, to agree, and to communicate the roles and responsibilities. The RACI model is a relatively straightforward tool that can be used for identifying roles and responsibilities during an organizational change process. Instead of the terminology RACI, sometimes also the concepts RASCI or RASIC are used.

Strategic Investments as Financial Options

Real Options capture the value of managerial flexibility to adapt strategic decisions in response to unexpected market developments. A company creates shareholder value by identifying Real Options, managing of Real Options, and exercising Real Options, associated with its investment portfolio. The Real Options method applies financial options theory to quantify the value of management flexibility, thus turning uncertainty to its advantage in a changing world.

The idea of treating strategic investments as financial options was conceived by Timothy A. Luehrman in two Harvard Business Review articles: "Investment Opportunities as Real Options: Getting Started on the Numbers" (July - August 1998) and "Strategy as a Portfolio of Real Options" (September - October 1998). In the last article Luehrman says: "In financial terms, a business strategy is much more like a series of options than a series of static cash flows". The following variables determine the option value:

1. *Time to expiration (duration).*
2. *Degree of uncertainty.*
3. *Cost of acquiring the option(s).*
4. *Potential cash flows lost, compared to full upfront commitment.*
5. *Risk-free interest rate.*
6. *Expected present value of future cash flows.*

By introducing these factors into business decision-making, the Real Options method has enabled corporate decision-makers to use uncertainty for the advantage of the firm and to create a limit to downside risk.

Team Management Profile

Traditionally, the individual reflected the quality of an organization. Increasingly, however, the organization is being measured by the team. The Team Management Profile, -Wheel and -Index (™) from Dr Charles J. Margerison and Dr Dick J. McCann constitute a method particularly useful for assessing work preferences in team context, and can also be used for assessing individual and organizational preferences. According to Margerison and McCann a good team has nine essential characteristics:

1. *Advising. Gathering and reporting information.*
2. *Innovating. Creating and experimenting with ideas.*
3. *Promoting. Exploring and presenting opportunities.*
4. *Developing. Assessing and testing the applicability of*

new approaches.
5. *Organizing. Establishing and implementing ways of "making things work".*
6. *Producing. Concluding and delivering outputs.*
7. *Inspecting. Controlling and auditing the working of systems.*
8. *Maintaining. Upholding and safeguarding standards and processes.*
9. *Linking. Coordinating and integrating the work of others.*

This provides eight team role preferences that people can perform in the Team Management Wheel :

1. *Reporter / Adviser. Supporter, helper, tolerant; a collector of information; he dislikes being rushed; knowledgeable; flexible.*
2. *Creator / Innovator. Imaginative; future-oriented; enjoys complexity; creative; likes research work.*
3. *Explorer / Promoter. Persuades, likes varied, exciting, stimulating work; easily bored; influential and outgoing.*
4. *Assessor / Developer. Analytical and objective; developer of ideas; enjoys prototype or project work; experimenter.*
5. *Thruster / Organizer. Organizes and implements; quick to decide; results-oriented; sets up systems; analytical.*
6. *Concluder / Producer. Practical; production-oriented; likes schedules and plans; pride in reproducing goods and services; values effectiveness and efficiency.*

7. *Controller / Inspector. Strong on control; detail-oriented; low need for people contact; an inspector of standards and procedures.*
8. *Upholder / Maintainer. Conservative, loyal, supportive; personal values important; strong sense of right and wrong; work motivation based on purpose.*

Appreciative Inquiry

Appreciative Inquiry is about the co-evolutionary search for the best in people, their organizations, and the relevant world around them. AI asks the questions that strengthen a system's capacity to apprehend, anticipate, and heighten positive potential. The following are the five basic principles of Appreciative Inquiry:

1. *Constructionist Principle. To be effective as executives, leaders, change agents, etc., we must be adept in the art of understanding, reading, and analyzing organizations as living, human constructions.*
2. *Principle of Simultaneity. Here it is recognized that inquiry and change are not truly separate moments, but are simultaneous.*
3. *Poetic Principle. A metaphor here is that human organizations are like an open book. An organization's story is constantly being co-authored. We can inquire into the nature of alienation or joy, enthusiasm or low morale, efficiency or excess, in any human organization.*
4. *Anticipatory Principle. Constructive organizational change generates from th e infinite human resource we call our collective imagination and discourse about the*

future.

5. *Positive Principle. We are more effective the longer we can retain the spirit of inquiry of the everlasting beginner. Things like hope, excitement, inspiration, caring, camaraderie, a sense of urgent purpose create joy when we build something meaningful together.*

The Appreciative Inquiry process is broken into four steps:

1. *Discovery. Mobilizing a whole system inquiry into the positive change core.*
2. *Dream. Creating a vision in relation to discovered potential and in relation to questions of higher purpose, i.e., "What is the world calling us to become?"*
3. *Design. Creating the ideal organization.*
4. *Destiny. Strengthening the affirmative capability of the whole system enabling it to build hope and momentum around a deep purpose.*

Catalytic Mechanisms

Catalytic Mechanisms are simple managerial tools, originally described by Jim Collins, which can help organizations to turn goals into results. They galvanize business devices that translate lofty aspirations into concrete reality. Catalytic Mechanisms have five distinct characteristics:

1. *A catalytic mechanism produces desired results in unpredictable ways.*
2. *A catalytic mechanism distributes power for the benefit of the overall system, often to the great discomfort of those who traditionally hold power.*

3. *A catalytic mechanism has teeth. In contrast to lofty aspirations, a catalytic mechanism puts a process in place that all but guarantees that the vision will be fulfilled.*
4. *A catalytic mechanism ejects viruses. In contrast to traditional controls that are designed to get employees to act in the right way, catalytic mechanisms help organizations to assemble the right people in the first place, keep them, and eject those who do not share the company's core values.*
5. *A catalytic mechanism produces an ongoing effect. Unlike electrifying off-site meetings, exciting strategic initiatives, or impending crisis, a good catalytic mechanism can last for decades.*

There are five steps in the Catalytic Mechanisms process:

1. *Don't just add, remove. Break the natural inclination to add new initiatives, new systems, new strategies, new priorities, and new catalytic mechanisms. Taking something away can be as catalytic as adding something new.*
2. *Create, don't copy. You can get good ideas by looking at what other organizations do, but the best catalytic mechanisms are idiosyncratic adaptations.*
3. *Make use of money, but not only money. Research shows that only about half of catalytic mechanisms use money. To rely entirely on money reflects shallow understanding of human behavior.*
4. *Allow your mechanisms to evolve. New catalytic mechanisms sometimes produce unintended negative*

consequences and need correction.

5. *Build an integrated set of catalytic mechanisms. One catalytic mechanism is good; several that reinforce one another as a set is even better. That's not to say that a company needs hundreds of catalytic mechanisms - a handful will do.*

Change Equation

Historically, the Change Equation can be seen as a major milestone for the field of Organizational Development. Employers not only want to move their organizations forward in terms of business objectives, but also in terms of employee engagement. Today's employers now understand the connection between employee involvement and organizational success.

The move to employee involvement in change, and the use of internal or external consultants to manage reactions to change, represents a shift in thinking from earlier management theory, such as Charles Taylor's scientific management approach, which became known as Taylorism. This "command - and-control" approach drew a sharp line between managers and employees. The underlying philosophy was that "workers work, and managers think."

The Change Equation can help one understand that all three of the following components must be present to overcome the resistance to change in an organization:

1. *Dissatisfaction with the present situation,*
2. *Vision of what is possible in the future, and*

3. *Achievable first steps towards reaching this vision.*

If any of the three is zero or near zero, the product will also be zero or near zero and the resistance to change will dominate.

Disruptive Innovation

The Disruptive Innovation model from Clayton Christensen is a theory that describes the impact of new technologies (revolutionary change) on a firm's existence. Clayton Christensen first coined the phrase "disruptive technologies" in 1997, in his book "The Innovator's Dilemma: When New Technologies Cause Great Firms to Fail ". He showed that time and again almost all the organizations that have "died" or been displaced from their industries (because of a new paradigm of customer offering) could see the disruption coming, but did nothing until it was too late.

When companies cater to their most profitable customers and focus investments where profit margins are most attractive - established industry leaders are on a path of sustaining innovations and leave themselves open for disruptive technologies to bury them. This happens because the resource allocation processes of established companies are designed to maximize profits through sustaining innovations, which essentially involve designing better and better mousetraps for existing customers or proven market segments.

When Disruptive Innovations (typically cheaper, simpler to use versions of existing products that target low-end or entirely new customers) emerge, established companies are paralyzed. They are almost always motivated to go up-market rather than to defend these new or low-end markets, and ultimately the disruptive innovation improves, steals more market share, and replaces the reigning product.

Redesigning Organizational Processes

The Business Process Reengineering method (BPR) is described by Michael Hammer and James Champy as "the fundamental reconsideration and the radical redesign of organizational processes, in order to achieve drastic improvement of current performance in cost, services and speed." Rather than organizing a firm into functional specialties (like production, accounting, marketing, etc.) and to look at the tasks that each function performs, Hammer and Champy recommend that we should rebuild the firm into a series of processes, from materials acquisition, towards production, towards marketing and distribution. The authors describe a five step approach to business process reengineering:

1. *Develop the business vision and process objectives: The BPR method is driven by a business vision that implies specific business objectives such as cost reduction, time reduction, output quality improvement.*

2. *Identify the business processes to be redesigned: most firms use the 'high-impact' approach that focuses on the most important processes or those that conflict most with the business vision. A lesser number of firms use the 'exhaustive approach' that attempts to identify all the processes within an organization and then prioritize*

them in order of redesign urgency.
3. Understand and measure the existing processes: to avoid the repeating of old mistakes and to provide a baseline for future improvements.
4. Identify IT levers: awareness of IT capabilities can and should influence BPR.
5. Design and build a prototype of the new process: the actual design should not be viewed as the end of the BPR process. Rather, it should be viewed as a prototype, with successive iterations. The metaphor of prototype aligns the Business Process Reengineering approach with quick delivery of results, and the involvement.

Information Warfare (OODA)

This is an information strategy concept for information warfare developed by Colonel John Boyd, a fighter pilot (1927 - 97). Although the model was clearly created for military purposes, elements of the theory can also be applied to business strategy called observe, orient, decide and act.

Basically it is acting through a decision making process based on observations of the world around you. The enemy will observe unfolding circumstances and gather outside information in order to orient the system to perceived threats. Colonel Boyd concludes the orientation phase is the most important because if the enemy perceives the wrong threats, or misunderstands what is happening in the environment, then he will orient his thinking (and forces) in wrong directions and ultimately make incorrect decisions.

Further, by attacking the thought process of the

enemy/competitor, his morale and decision process can be shattered.

Identifying Sources of Power

The Bases of Social Power is a theory developed by French and Raven. This theory identifies six sources of social (organizational) power:

1. *Reward power: Based on the ability to give positive consequences or remove negative ones.*

2. *Coercive power: This is the perceived ability to punish nonconformists.*

3. *Legitimate power: Someone is authorized to direct and command.*

4. *Referent power: Power achieved through association with others.*

5. *Expert power: Based on having distinctive knowledge or expertise.*

6. *Information power: Information needed by others in order to reach a goal.*

This theory argues that the reaction of the receiving agent is the more useful focus for explaining the phenomena of social influence and power. Attraction and resistance are the recipient's sentiment towards the agent that uses power.

Constraint Management

This is a theory developed by Eliyahu Goldratt. The author describes several thinking processes and their applications.

Cause and Effect:

Central to the concept is the acknowledgement of cause and effect. The process gives us a series of steps, which combine cause- effect and our experience and intuition. To the existing complexity of any business organization when you add to the dynamic of changing customers, suppliers, workforce, regulations, etc., you have a picture of the challenge faced by today's management team.

Traditionally management has divided the organization into smaller, more manageable pieces. The object is to maximize the performance of each part. The global improvement is assumed to be equal to the sum of the local improvements. The Theory of Constraints involves the following steps:

1   Identify your constraint.
2   Focus on the Constraint. A company must first know its goal and the necessary conditions for achievement.
3   Follow it through. The process of ongoing improvement. Identify the constraint and exploit it.
4   Subordinate all other operations to the necessity to exploit the constraint
5   Go back to #1. but don't let inertia become the system's constraint.

Predicting Innovation Curves

The Bass Diffusion Model, developed by Frank M. Bass, is one of the tools to describe, and sometimes predict, the number of purchases for new consumer durable products. The spread of a new concept in a market can be characterized by the Bass formula:

$$N_t = N_{t-1} + p\left(m - N_{t-1}\right) + q\,\frac{N_{t-1}}{m}\left(m - N_{t-1}\right)$$

There are three parameters to predict Nt (number of adopters at time t):

1. m = market potential – total number of people who will eventually use the product
2. p = coefficient of innovation (external influence) – the likelihood that someone who is not presently using the product will because of media or other external factors
3. q = coefficient of imitation (internal influence) – the likelihood that someone who is not presently using the product will because of word of mouth from one who is already using it

Bass Diffusion theory is simple enough to allow a first assessment. However, care must be taken to be aware of which variation is being used, as there are many. For new products or early stage investments, it is necessary to have some understanding of the likely diffusion. Otherwise, a company could misjudge how much time and capital should be invested.

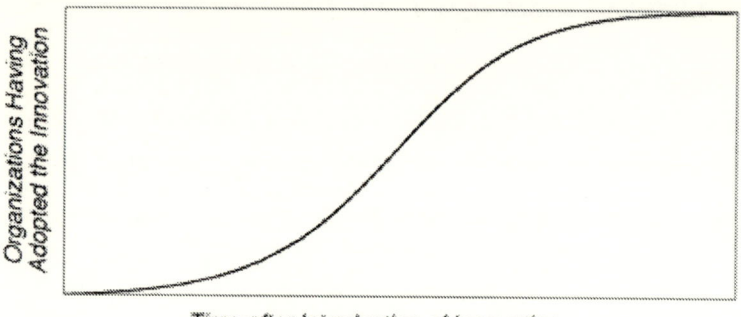

Figure 7.3

The Generative Dance Towards Knowledge Creation that Bridges the Epistemologies of Possession and Action

The Bridging Epistemo logies Model of S.D.N. Cook and J.S. Brown argues that organizational knowledge is based on a single, traditional understanding of the nature of knowledge. Actions by collectives cannot be reduced to only the actions of individuals within them. Cook and Brown identify 4 types of knowledge: explicit and tacit at both the individual and collective levels. The term 'generative dance' describes the process by which different knowledge types are used. Knowledge creation does not simply rely on an inventory of knowledge elements (possession), but on the ability to use those as tools (action).

This framework helps us to think of knowledge in an organizational context and to understand why and how we know things collectively. According to Cook and Brown, ways of 'knowing' reflected in workers' interactions with each other and their work are as essential for product development as are forms of knowledge distributed among individuals and groups. Following is an example of the Bridging Epistemologies model using a bakery:

- *Knowledge as concepts – theory known by individuals, such as which flour to use, etc.*
- *Skills – the ability to bake bread*
- *Stories – how things were built up*
- *Genre – the context of the bakery*

An apprentice can learn all of these elements, but he/she will need experience in order to make bread: knowledge as action.

Preventing Common Mistakes in Change Processes

According to John Kotter in his book, "A Force for Change: How Leadership Differs from Management" (1990), failing to build a substantial coalition, and failing to understand and communicate a clear vision, among other things, leads to failed change processes. To prevent this from happening, Kotter created the following Change Phases model:

1. *Establish a sense of urgency.*
2. *Create a coalition.*
3. *Develop a clear vision.*
4. *Share the vision.*
5. *Empower people to clear obstacles from that vision.*
6. *Secure short-term wins.*
7. *Consolidate and keep moving.*
8. *Anchor the change.*

According to Kotter, it is crucial to follow the above steps in their exact sequence.

Thesis, Antithesis and Synthesis

Dialectic Inquiry, or Dialectics, the idea that everything is made of opposites, has a long history in many cultures. Later the distinction between Thesis, Antithesis and Synthesis was clarified in Hegel's work and subsequently extended by Marx and Engels.

There are several definitions of Dialectics, however, the above graph can help one appreciate the important difference between dialectics and a trade-off (mix), a dilemma, a puzzle, and an average. Strategy, Management and Business Ethics are all complex by nature. Dialectics offers a number of advantages. DeWit and Meyer mentions the following advantages of taking a dialectical approach (instead of treating the tensions as puzzles, dilemmas, trade-offs or taking the average):

- *A range of ideas can be exploited*
- *Helps focus on points of contention*
- *Provides a stimulus for bridging what seem like irreconcilable opposites*
- *Provides a stimulus for creativity*

Regression Analysis Method

Dynamic Regression is a statistical model that helps businesses to make forecasts. It includes lagged values of explanatory variables or of dependent variables, or both. Such a model can predict what will happen if the explanatory variable changes.

Dynamic Regression is similar to Regression Analysis,

but is believed to produce more realistic results because it emphasizes ripple effects that input variables can have on the dependent variable.

Uncovering the Underlying Structure of a Large Set of Variables

In 1935, Thurstone's book, "Vectors of Mind," presented the mathematical and logical basis for the theory of Exploratory Factor Analysis, a technique that can be used to reduce a large set of variables to a couple of underlying factors. For example, you have set up a questionnaire about customer satisfaction in the civil aviation industry, identifying 30 items to describe and evaluate customer satisfaction. By using EFA, you can reduce the set of 30 items within your analyzing process to a couple of central factors that underlay your set of items. Statistical packages, such as SPSS or SAS, can be used to analyze EFA data.

EFA can be used for customer satisfaction surveys, measuring service quality, personality tests, image surveys, identifying market segments, and typing customers, products or behavior. Briefly, here are the steps in Exploratory Factor Analysis:

1. *Identify the items that go in the EFA.*
2. *Calculate a correlation matrix (coefficient of correlation from Bravais-Pearson).*
3. *Examine the correlation matrix to be used for an EFA.*
4. *Choose a factor extraction method.*
5. *Discover the factors and the factor loadings (factor loadings are the correlation coefficients between*

the variables and factors).
6. Fix the number of factors to be extracted (it is useful to take the Kaiser-Criteria and the Scree -Test with the elbow-criteria).
7. Interpret the factors extracted.

EFA is easy to use, it is useful for lots of survey questions, is the basis of other instruments, and is easy to combine with other instruments.

Supply Chain Planning

The Just-in-Time philosophy arose out of Japan's desire to improve its production quality by minimizing inventories and increasing response to customer needs. JIT was pioneered by Taiichi Ohno at the Toyota assembly plants in Japan. At the heart of JIT is the kanban, the Japanese word for card. The kanban card is sent to the warehouse to request parts only when they are needed. This technique is used mainly for high - volume repetitive flow manufacturing processes.

Typical attention areas of JIT include: inventory reduction, smaller production lots and batch sizes, quality control, complexity reduction and transparency, flat organization structure and delegation, and waste minimization. With the arrival of Internet and Supply Chain Planning software, companies are able to streamline manufacturing, ordering and delivery processes even more.

Measuring and Accounting Intellectual Capital

Measuring and Accounting Intellectual Capital (MAGIC) is a research and development project funded by the

European Commission to develop a methodology and measurement system for Intellectual Capital. A software system has been developed to support the implementation of a measurement system for intangible assets. Four categories of the MAGIC method are:

1. *Human capital* – *the sum of all the skills and expertise of a company to react on market demands and customer needs, and includes leadership and management issues and capabilities.*
2. *Organizational capital* – *the total of a company's ability to create products and services for the market.*
3. *Market capital* – *represents a company's ability to interact with customers, partners, suppliers, and other stakeholders.*
4. *Innovation capital* – *refers to a company's ability to innovate, improve and develop non-utilized potential, as well as generate long-term wealth.*

Measuring and Accounting Intellectual Capital

Measuring and Accounting Intellectual Capital (MAGIC) is a research and development project funded by the European Commission to develop a methodology and measurement system for Intellectual Capital. A software system has been developed to support the implementation of a measurement system for intangible assets. Four categories of the MAGIC method are:

1. *Human capital* – *the sum of all the skills and expertise of a company to react on market demands and customer*

needs, and includes leadership and management issues and capabilities.
2. *Organizational capital* – the total of a company's ability to create products and services for the market.
3. *Market capital* – represents a company's ability to interact with customers, partners, suppliers, and other stakeholders.
4. *Innovation capital* – refers to a company's ability to innovate, improve and develop non-utilized potential, as well as generate long -term wealth.

Defining Objectives for Employees and Directing their Performance against these Objectives

Management by Objectives (MBO) was first outlined in 1954 by Peter Drucker in his book "The Practice of Management." MBO works by defining objectives for each employee and then comparing and directing their performance against objectives that have been set. The goal is to increase organization productivity by matching organization objectives with those of employees, providing feedback to achieve such. Principles of MBO are:

1. *Cascading of organizational goals and objectives*
2. *Specific objectives for each member*
3. *Participation in decision making*
4. *Explicit time period*
5. *Performance evaluation and feedback*

Management by Objectives uses the SMART method to check objective validity: Specific, Measurable, Achievable, Realistic, and Time-related. In order for MBO to work, objectives must be known.

Explanation of Organizational Learning

There are many definitions of Organizational Learning, but a 'learning organization' is a firm that purposefully constructs structures and strategies to enhance and maximize Organizational Learning. OL is more than the sum of the parts of individual learning. When members leave an organization, that organization does not lose out on its learning abilities, due to the accumulation of histories, experiences and stories. Although, creating an unlearning organization is just as important as creating a learning one, since at times an organization must forget some of its past. According to Chris Argyris and Donald Schön, there are three types of Organizational Learning:

1. *Single-loop learning – when errors are detected and corrected, and firms continue with their present policies and goals. It can be equated to activities that add to the knowledge base without altering the fundamental nature of the firm's activities.*
2. *Double-loop learning – in addition to detection and correction, the organization questions and modifies existing norms, procedures, policies, and objectives. It involves changing the organization's knowledge base.*
3. *Deutero-learning – when both Single-loop and Double-loop learning is employed. These first two forms of learning will not happen if an organization is not aware that learning must occur.*

Double-loop and Deutero-learning are concerned with the why and how to change the organization, while Single-loop is concerned with accepting change without questioning underlying assumptions and core beliefs. The type of Organizational Learning chosen depends on where in the organization the learning occurs.

Information Retention, Acquisition, and Retrieval in an Organization

The origins of the Organizational Memory method from Walsh and Ungson are based upon the work of early 20 th century scholars such as Durkheim and Vygotsky. The method is used for information retention, acquisition, and retrieval in an organization. According to Walsh and Ungson, organizational memory can be classified within six information "storage bins":

1. *Individuals*
2. *Culture (stories, mental models)*
3. *Transformations (various processes and procedures)*
4. *Structures (roles within the organization)*
5. *Ecology (physical setting of organization)*
6. *External archives (information documentation)*

Information in organizational memory is distributed across different facilities, not centrally stored. Organizational memory gives a simple framework to guide HR in improving knowledge management. It allows institutions to benefit from historical information despite the transient nature of organizational membership. It can serve as a competitive advantage and can actually reduce transaction costs. Finally, it can serve a political role in organizations.

Alternatively, placing too much emphasis on

organizational memory can disable learning in an organization, causing rigidity; a company may no longer notice changes in the environment. Artifacts such as roles and organizational structure may also become impediments to change.

Scanning the External Macro-environment in which a Firm Operates

PEST Analysis is a framework that strategy consultants use to scan the external macro-environment in which a firm operates. It plays an important role in a strategy's opportunity to create value. PEST stands for the following factors: Political, Economic, Social and Technological. These are normally outside corporation control and must be considered as either threats or opportunities.

Some examples of PEST Analysis are: environmental regulations and protection, income distribution, tax policies, population growth rates, government spending, consumer protection, employment laws, exchange rates, energy use and cost, inflation rates, political stability, safety regulations, and consumer confidence.

Completing a PEST Analysis is relatively simple and usage can be in the form of company and strategic planning, marketing planning, business and product development, and research reports.

Aligning Business and Information Strategy

The Strategic Alignment Model of Venka Traman, Henderson and Oldach, a framework for aligning business strategy and IT strategy, argues that there is a lack of alignment between these two strategies, and also that there is a lack of dynamic administrative process to ensure such alignment, leading to difficulty in realizing value from IT investments. Four dominant alignment perspectives are described:

1. Strategy Execution – views the business strategy as the driver of both organization design choices and IT infrastructure logic.
2. Technology Potential – also views the business strategy as the driver. However, it involves the formulation of an IT strategy to support the chosen business strategy and the corresponding specification of the required IT infrastructure and processes.
3. Competitive Potential – is concerned with the exploitation of emerging IT capabilities to:
   1. Impact new products and services
   2. Influence key attributes of strategy
   3. Develop new forms of relationships
4. This perspective allows the modification of business strategy via emerging IT capabilities.
5. Service level – focuses on how to build a world class IT organization within an organization. Here the role of business strategy is indirect. This perspective is often viewed as being necessary but not sufficient to ensure the effective use of IT resources and to be responsive to the growing and quickly changing demands of the end - user population.

Second Generation Performance Management

Because of the significant weaknesses of first generation performance measurement frameworks, Andrew Jack developed a second generation Performance Management Model. There is a great need in organizations to report more effectively on the creation of value for their stakeholders. Using Value Mapping, management can identify the most important stakeholder needs and subsequently use these to measure value outcomes as well as develop an integrated strategy.

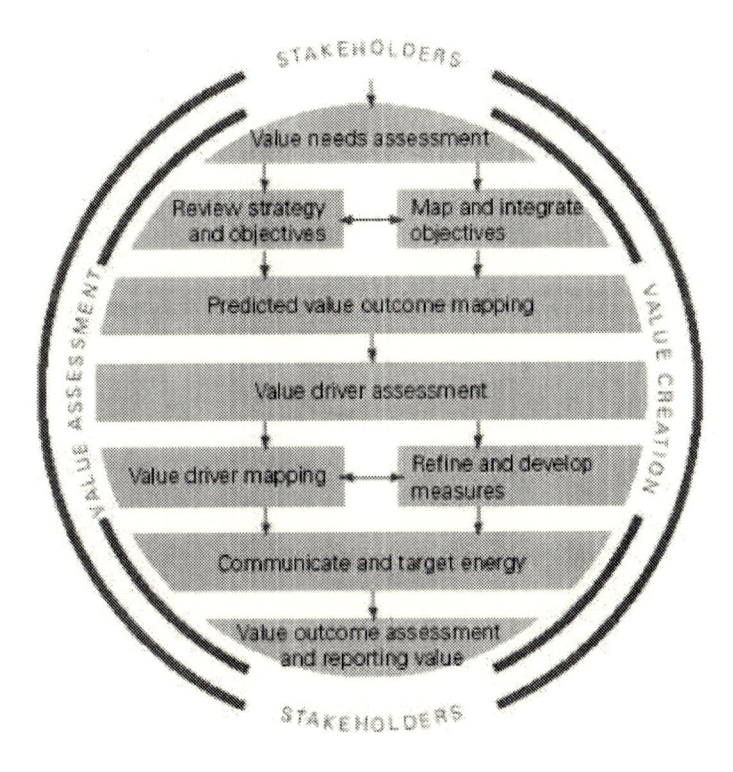

Figure 7.4

Translating Customer Needs into Actions and Designs to Build and Deliver a Quality Product

The Quality Function Deployment (QFD) philosophy was first developed in Japan in the late 1960s by Yoji Akao and Shigeru Mizuno, who wanted to develop a quality assurance method that would design customer satisfaction into a product before it was manufactured. QFD was introduced to America and Europe beginning in 1983.

QFD uses diagrams, matrixes, and blueprinting to accomplish its goal. Special note should be made of the House of Quality, a conceptual map that starts with customer needs, which form the base of the house. Corresponding engineering characteristics are specified and now interdependencies are mapped, which form the roof of the house. Technical difficulties in achieving the desired changes are calculated. The final output is a set of target values for each technical requirement to be met by the new design, which are linked back to the demands of the customer. Typically, a QFD process has the following stages:

1. *Derive top level product requirements or technical characteristics from customer needs acquired through market surveys.*
2. *Develop product concepts to satisfy these requirements.*
3. *Evaluate product concepts to select the most optimal.*
4. *Partition the system concept into subsystems and transfer higher level requirements to these subsystems.*
5. *Derive lower-level product requirements from subsystem/assembly requirements.*
6. *For critical assemblies, derive lower -level product requirements into process planning.*
7. *Determine manufacturing process steps that correspond to these assembly characteristics.*
8. *Determine set-up requirements, process and quality*

controls to assure achievement of these critical assembly characteristics.

QFD seeks out customer requirements and focuses all product development activities on customer needs. It makes invisible requirements and strategic advantages visible, allowing companies to prioritize and deliver on them. It reduces time to market, design changes, and costs, while improving quality and customer satisfaction.

On the other hand, some problems can occur when QFD, developed under Japanese management techniques, is applied within the western business environment. And while customer needs are attained through market surveys, it must be kept in mind that, in order to be useful, the survey must be performed properly. Customer needs and wants change quickly. Comprehensive system and methodical thinking can make adapting to changed market needs more complex.

Chapter 8 - Finance and Investments

"Sometimes your best investments are the ones you don't make - Donald Trump 1946"-, American Businessman

Cash Flow from Operations (Operating Cash flow)

This refers to the quality of a company's earnings. It is used to determine the extent to which cash flow differs from the reported level of either Operating Income or Net Income. In other words, it is a check on the quality of the company's earnings. It is a better measure than profits earnings because a company can show positive net earnings and still not be able to pay its debt.

The cash flow can be determined by two formats. One way is to divide operational cash flow by income from operations. The other method is to divide the cash flow from all transactions by net income.

Both calculations measure the cash generated from operations, not counting capital spending or working capital requirements. This has obvious benefits in that these are honest ways to positively portray the company's financial state despite various circumstances that might otherwise appear to lead to a negative assessment.

Measuring Liquidity (Explanation of Cash ratio)

This is a formula for measuring the liquidity of a company by calculating the ratio between all cash and cash equivalent assets and all current liabilities. It excludes both inventory and accounts receivables in the Current Ratio. A key element of this formula is that it ignores the timing of both cash received and cash paid out.

The formula is an indicator of the extent to which a company can pay its current liabilities with selling inventory or considering accounts receivable. This is an important barometer of the company's capacity to liquidate its assets.

Return on Investment

This is an accounting valuation method. Basically it is book income as a proportion of net book value. It is the return ratio that compares the net benefits of a project, versus its total costs.

Because the numerator (net income) is unreliable the outcome of the formula for ROI must also be unreliable. In fat, Return on Equity overstates economic value. To what extent? That will depend on the following five factors:

1. *Length of project life. The longer it is, the larger the overstatement.*
2. *Capitalization policy. If the factor of the total investment is smaller, the overstatement will be larger.*
3. *Rate at which depreciation is taken in the books. If the depreciation rate is faster than the straight line basis, the result will be a higher ROI*
4. *Lag between outlays and earning back the outlays. If the lag is greater, the overstatement will be greater.*
5. *Growth rate of new investment. Fast growing companies will have lower ROI.*

Return on Net Assets (Return on Net Assets, RONA)

RONA is a method for measuring company success. It

is equal to the Net Operating Profit (after tax) divided by cash plus the working capital requirements.

This method does not explicitly measure capital charges, but it does remind managers that there is a cost to acquiring and holding assets. This is important if they are to keep a clear vision of the company's overall financial picture. The formula for calculating RONA takes into account net sales, operating expenses, operating profits, and taxes.

Debt to Equity

Sometimes there is the need to research and measure the solvency and capital structure of a company. The Dept to Equity approach is one way of accomplishing this. This method indicates the extent to which the company is leveraged (i.e., in debt) by comparing what is owed to what is owned.

Creditors and investors keep a watchful eye on a company's debt to equity ratio because it reveals the willingness of the company's management is to fund its operations with debt rather than using equity. This can provide investors with invaluable insights into the company's financial thinking.

The debt to equity ratio is calculated by dividing the total debt (total liabilities) by total equity. This figure can then be multiplied by 100 to get a percentage.

Determining the Accounting Value (Return on Equity)

This is an accounting method that measures how efficiently a company uses its assets to produce earnings. It takes into consideration that some companies are more efficient than others when it comes to using their assets to produce earnings.

Because the numerator (Net Income) is an unreliable corporate performance measurement, the outcome of the formula for ROE cannot be relied upon to determine success or corporate value. Nonetheless, the formula still shows up in many annual reports.

Portfolio Management

The Arthur D. Little Company has developed a Portfolio Management model based on the industry life cycle. This approach uses an industry assessment and a business strength assessment as its dimensions. The business strength measure is a categorization of the corporation's SBU's into one of five competitive positions: dominant, strong, favorable, tenable, weak and nonviable. This yields a matrix of five competitive positions amidst the four life cycle stages. Positioning in the matrix identifies a general strategy. A line of business is defined by the following:

1. Common rivals
2. Prices
3. Customers
4. Quality/Style
5. Substitutability
6. Divestment of industries

This model assesses the industry life cycle stages using the following criteria:

1. Business market share
2. Investment
3. Profitability and cash flow

Like all methods, this one has its limitations. Primarily, these include the lack of a standard life cycle length, and the influence of competitors upon this length.

Predicting Bankruptcy: The Z Score Formula

Edward Altman has developed a multivariate formula for a measurement of the financial health of a company known as the Z Score Formula. It is a powerful tool to diagnose the probability that a company will go bankrupt within a 2 - year period. Studies measuring the effectiveness of the Z score have shown the model is often accurate in predicting bankruptcy (72% - 80 %).

The Z score is not a crystal ball, or a rough guess. It's a carefully thought out formula that combines the five common business ratios, using a weighting system calculated by Altman. Thus it determines the likelihood that a company will go bankrupt. It was derived based on data from manufacturing firms but has since proven to also be effective (with some modifications) in determining the risk that a services firm will go bankrupt.

The scores vary depending on the kind of company being evaluated. For example, if a public manufacturing company's Z score is 3.0 or above, bankruptcy is not likely. At the other extreme, if the score is 1.8 or less, bankruptcy is likely. For private manufacturing companies, however, the numbers change, respectively, to 2.90 and 1.23.

Quantifying the Link Between an Organizations' Non-financial Performance and its Valuation in the Markets(Value Creation Index of CGE&Y)

This index is a tool designed to quantify the link between an organization's non-financial performance and its valuation in the markets. These financial factors are quite important, yet assigning values for them often proves difficult to quantify. Moreover (precisely because they are "non-financial") they are rarely acknowledged in accounting methods.

This index not only quantifies the impact of the non-financial performance on market value, but also identifies the specific intangibles that drive the success (or failure) of companies within various industries. The factors taken into account include:

1 Innovation.
2 Customer relations.
3 Management capabilities.
4 Alliances.
5 Technology.
6 Brand value.
7 Employee relations.
8 Environmental and community issues.

Allocating a Firm's Financial Resources across its Strategic Business Units

The STRATPORT, Strategic Portfolio Planning, model of Larreche and Srinivasan (81 -82) is an online computerized mathematical decision support model that utilizes empirical and managerial judgment based data.

It is a decision support system for the allocation of a firm's financial resources across its Strategic Business Units (portfolio analysis). The system can evaluate the profit and cash flow implications. Alternatively, the approach can determine the optimal allocation of marketing expenditures across Strategic business Units in order to maximize net present value over a specified time horizon.

There are similar models that use slightly different approaches. For example, in the GE Matrix formula, the business units are classified into nine groups according to company strength and industry attractiveness. The position of a given business unit on each of these dimensions is determined qualitatively from a number of market competitive, environmental and internal factors.

Explanation of Value Disciplines

According to authors Michael Treacy and Fred Wiersema, there are four new rules (known as value disciplines) that companies must obey if they want to be competitive market leaders:

1. *Provide the best offer in the marketplace, by excelling in one dimension of value.*
2. *Maintain threshold standards on other dimensions of value.*
3. *Dominate your market by improving the value, year after year.*
4. *Build a well-tuned operating model dedicated to delivering unmatched value in a competitive marketplace. Be a market leader.*

The authors describe three generic value disciplines. Any company must choose one of these three and act upon it:

1. *Operational Excellence:* Superb operations and execution.
2. *Product Leadership:* Very strong in innovation and brand marketing. Focus on development, innovation, design, time to market, high margins in a short time frame.
3. *Customer Intimacy:* Company excels in customer attention and customer service. Tailors its products and services to individual or prospective individual customers. Focus on delivering products on time and exceeding customer expectations.

With the increased competition of today's marketplace, adherence to these principles is more important than ever. Any company that fails to do so risks falling behind and giving a competitive edge to its adversaries.

Activity Based Costing (ABC)

This is a departure from the traditional cost accounting methods, which are mostly based on volume. Regular cost accounting makes some assumptions, which might not necessarily be true, like high volume customers are profitable. Why? Too much may have to be given to them for the volume of business they provide, which reduces the per unit profit. By using ABC, a manufacturer can identify the most profitable customers, products and channels. ABC allows managers to know exactly what the product costs them in terms of material, labor, and marketing. One of the most immediate benefits of this system is giving the manager the tools he needs to analyze cost and to find out what things his workers are doing that add value and those things that don't add value.

Let's take a look at how ABC can be superior. Managers no longer rely on time consuming and costly employee surveys where an employee hands in a survey in which he estimates where his time is spent. Of course, in a practical sense the employee does this to a certain degree tongue in cheek, as his estimate accounts for 100% of his time. He didn't talk about the thirty idle minutes he sat at his station, chatting with others, as he waited for manufacturing components to arrive. He didn't talk about taking an extra ten minutes at morning and afternoon break.

Another example is that the ABC model enables a manager to approximate the complexity of the manufacturing operation by showing what causes variations in processing times, allowing him/her to track costs of activities and work processes on the assembly line. This type of progressive accounting (ABC) will also enable the manufacturer to achieve a better marketing mix. Let's assume that the product is a battery operated can opener, which cuts around the edge of the can and eliminates dangerous sharp edges. Most of the marketing involves distribution through retail chains. But for certain customers, department store or other mass retail distribution might be inferior to TV advertising and selling by mail. Maybe many people who buy such can openers are elderly, have trouble using manual can openers and can't easily get out to shop. So it can be seen, that as suggested the profitable customer has been identified as well as the channel of distribution. ABC makes this possible.

Result Oriented Management

This is a management style described by Jan Schouten and Wim van Beers. The system achieves maximum results based on clear and measurable agreements made previously. People will work with more enthusiasm if:

1 They clearly know what is expected of them.
2 They are involved in establishing these expectations.
3 They are allowed to determine themselves how they are going to meet these expectations.

So-called Result Oriented Agreements are situations in which all parties have the same expectations about their target. All agreements must be "SMART, an acronym for Specific, Measurable Accepted Relevant and Traceable. The system helps translate corporate goals towards Strategic Business Units' goals and individual goals and uses the following steps:

1 Set the target -- long term goals.
2 Translating the corporate goals towards individual goals.
3 Result Oriented Agreements -- about goals
4 Implementation – self-steering and management reporting. Periodic appraisals, progress control and adjustments.

Explanation of Cash Flow Return on Investment CFROI

As originally developed by Holt Value Associates, this

is an economic profit performance evaluation framework, mainly used by portfolio managers and corporation. It is usually circulated on an annual basis and is compared to an inflation adjusted cost of capital to determine whether the returns are superior to its cost of capital

A complex calculation it can be seen as an approximation of the verge real internal rate of return earned by a firm on all its operating assets The inflation adjusted CFROI is calculated from a recurring stream of after tax cash flows generated by a company's growing base of depreciating and non depreciating assets.

Inside out strategy: Explanation of Discounted Cash Flow

DCF is the amount someone is willing to pay today, in order to receive the anticipated cash flow of future years. This method converts future earnings to today's values so as to determine proper valuation of a company.

Here is how the DCF is calculated. Estimate the cash flow you will have to pay out and the cash which you expect to receive back. Each cash transaction must then be recalculated by subtracting the opportunity cost of capital between now and when you will receive the cash.

There are practical applications for this method. It shows where projected future cash flows are "discounted" by an interest rate that reflects the perceived risk of the cash flows. The discount rate reflects the time value (having it now rather than later) of money and the risk premium (compensation for the risk if the flow does not materialize.

Fair Value Accounting

This is an accounting expression, originally defined by the SEC. Under GAAP, the Fair Value of an asset is the amount at which that asset could be bought or sold in a current transaction between willing parties, other than in a liquidation. An estimate should be made by using the best information available.

Today's markets are dynamic and volatile. Whether it is for buying or selling, what people want to know is what an asset is worth today. This method provides more transparency than historical cost based measurements. This method might have avoided some of the losses that investors had during downturns in the economy.

Gross Profit Percentage

This is a ratio that can be derived from an income statement. GPP reveals the resulting profit from operations after all variable costs have been subtracted from revenues. It can be used for deterring the efficiency of the performance of a company because it shows the productions efficiency in relation to the prices and unit volumes at which products or services are sold.

The Gross Profit Percentage can be compared with other factors to glean meaningful information. Here are three examples:

1. Comparing the GPP ratio with an industry average to show relative performance.

2. Comparing the GPP between different divisions within an entity. This will show which divisions may

require further investigation.

3 *Comparing the GPP over time. Compare this year with last year. An increase in the ration may be an indication that the cost of sales is understated or that revenue is overstated. A decrease may indicate that cost of sales is overstated or that gross revenue is understated. Many times change is cause by a change in production methods, product mix or some other reason.*

GPP Ratio Calculation

Here is a common ratio calculation: Add together the cost of overhead, direct materials and direct labor: subtract the total from revenue: and then divide the result by revenue. A problem with this approach is that many of the production costs are not truly variable. To avoid this, it is necessary to use another calculation formula, which only includes direct materials, shifting the productions costs into operation and administrative areas.

Leveraged Buy-Out

This is a corporate finance method under which a company is acquired by a person or entity using the value of the company's assets to finance its acquisition. This allows the acquirer to minimize the outlay of cashing in making the purchase. In other words, an LBO is a method to acquire a company by which a business can seek to takeover another company or at least gain a controlling interest in that company.

Benefits of LBO:

1. *Low capital or cash requirement for the acquiring entity.*
2. *Synergy gains. By eliminating the value destroying effects of excessive diversification*
3. *Improved leadership and management. Some managers run companies in ways that improve their authority at the expense of the company's owners, shareholders and long term strength. The "discipline of debt" can force management to focus on certain initiatives such as divesting no-core businesses, downsizing, cost cutting or investing in technological upgrades that might otherwise be postponed or rejected outright.*
4. *Leveraging. As the debt ration increases, the equity portion of the acquisition financing shrinks to a level at which a private equity firm can acquire a company for 20-40% of the total purchase price.*

Leveraged buy-outs also have some inherent risks. One obvious risk of an LBO is that of financial distress and unforeseen events such as recession, litigation or changes in the regulatory environment.

Liquidation Value

Liquidation literally means turning the assets of a company into readily available cash. The liquidation value of an asset or company is" the estimated amount of money that it could be sold for quickly. There are two types of liquidation value:

1. *Orderly liquidation value. This assumes that the enterprise can afford to sell its assets to the highest*

bidder. It also assumes that the seller can take a reasonable amount of time to sell each asset.

2. *Distress liquidation value*. This is an "emergency" price. It is assumed that the enterprise must sell all its assets quickly for whatever it can sell them for.

(Note: The difference between the two values can be substantial).

The Corporation Reputation Quotient of Harris - Fobrun

This is a comprehensive measuring method of corporate reputation that was created specifically to capture the perceptions of any corporate stakeholder group such as consumers, investors, and employees. There are six "drivers" of the Corporate Reputation Quotient:

1. *Emotional Appeal: Good feeling about the company. Admiration and respect of the company.*

2. *Products and Services: Company believes in its products, offers high quality products. Develops innovative products, offers good value.*

3. *Vision and Leadership: Has excellent leadership, clear vision and recognizes market opportunism.*

4. *Workplace Environment: Is well managed, good place to work, has good employees.*

> 5. *Financial Performance: History of profitability, low risk investment, strong prospect for future. Tends to outperform competitors.*
>
> 6. *Social Responsibility: Supports good cause. Environmentally responsible. Treats people well.*

Dividend Payout Ratio

The Dividend Payout Ratio determines whether a company is generating a sufficient level of cash flow to assure a continued stream of dividends to its investors. It also measures the amount of current net income, which is paid out in dividends, instead of the amount retained by the business.

The Dividend Payout Ratio Formula (Cash Flow Measurement Formula) is relatively straightforward: Divide total annual dividend payments by annual Net Income plus Non-cash Expenses minus Non-cash Sales.

Calculating the Dividend Payout Ratio during one year provides a very unreliable indication only. A better approach is to run a trend line on the ratio during several years to see if a general pattern of decline or increase emerges. This ratio is useful in projecting the growth of company as well.

Earnings before Interest, Taxes and Depreciation

Earnings before interest, taxes, depreciation, and amortization, or EBITDA, came into wide use among private capital firms, wanting to calculate what they should pay for a business. The private capital firms that originally employed EBITDA as a useful valuation tool removed interest, taxes, depreciation, and amortization from their earnings calculations in order to replace them with their own presumably more precise numbers.

EBITDA is calculated via the following formula:

    Net Sales
-   *Operating Expenses*

    Operating Profit (EBIT)
+   *Depreciation Expenses*
+   *Amortization Expenses*

EBITDA

Investors also use EBITDA to measure the cash that public companies generate. EBITDA is often compared with cash flow, because it rightfully adds back to net income two major expense categories that have no impact on cash: depreciation and amortization.

Earnings per Share

Earnings per Share (EPS) has become the traditional method used for determining corporate value. Other words for EPS are: Accounting Earnings and Reported Earnings.

Earnings per Share can be calculated by subtracting the dividends on preferred stock from net income, and dividing the result by the (weighted average of the) combination of all outstanding common shares and all common stock equivalents. Six major reasons why EPS fails to reliably measure the economic value of firms are:

1. *Alternative accounting methods may be employed.*
2. *Risk is excluded. Both business risk and financial risk are not accounted for in annual reports.*
3. *Investment requirements are excluded. For example, changes in the working capital are not considered in Reported Earnings.*
4. *Dividend policy is not considered. For example, dividend decreases will show increased EPS but are in fact value neutral.*
5. *The time value of money is ignored. No present value calculation in Reported Earnings.*
6. *The increased role which intangible assets that have moved from an industrial economy towards a services and knowledge oriented economy.*

Economic Profit

Economic profit elaborates on Risk-Adjusted Return on Capital by incorporating the cost of equity capital. This is based on the market-required rate of return from holding a company's equity instruments, to assess whether shareholder wealth is being created.

Economic profit measures the return that is generated by each business line in excess of the cost of equity capital. Shareholder wealth is increased if capital can be employed at a return in excess of the bank's cost of equity capital. Similarly, when returns do not exceed the cost of equity capital, then shareholder wealth is diminished and a more effective deployment of that capital should be sought.

Economic Profit

Economic profit elaborate s on Risk-Adjusted Return On Capital by incorporating the cost of equity capital. This is based on the market-required rate of return from holding a company's equity instruments, to assess whether shareholder wealth is being created.

Economic profit measures the return that is generated by each business line in excess of the cost of equity capital. Shareholder wealth is increased if capital can be employed at a return in excess of the bank's cost of equity capital. Similarly, when returns do not exceed the cost of equity capital, then shareholder wealth is diminished and a more effective deployment of that capital should be sought.

Economic Value Added. (EVA)

Economic Value Added (EVA) uses a financial performance method to determine the true economic profit of a corporation. EVA can be calculated as Net Operating Profit After Tax (NOPAT) minus a charge for the opportunity cost of the capital invested.

The basic formula for calculating EVA is:

Net Sales
- *Operating Expenses*

Operating Profit
- Taxes

Net Operating Profit After Tax
- Capital Charges (Invested Capital x Cost of Capital)

Economic Value Added (EVA)

By taking all capital costs into account, including the cost of equity, EVA shows the financial amount of wealth a business has created or destroyed in a reporting period. In other words, EVA is profit in the way that shareholders define it. If the shareholders expect, say, a 10% return on their investment, they earn money only to the extent that their share of the NOPAT exceeds 10% of equity capital. Everything before that just builds up to the minimum acceptable compensation for investing in a risky enterprise.

Converting Future Earnings to Today's Money

Discounted Cash Flow (DCF) converts future earnings to today's money and is based on the sum someone is willing to pay today in order to receive the anticipated cash flow of future years. The DCF method recalculates future returns to represent their present values. In this way the value of a company or project under consideration as a whole is determined properly.

The DCF for an investment is calculated by estimating the cash that you will have to pay out and the cash that you expect to receive back. The timeframes that you expect to receive the payments must also be estimated. Each cash transaction must then be recalculated, by subtracting the opportunity cost of capital between now and the moment when you will pay or receive the cash.

For example, if inflation is 6%, the value of your money would halved every 12 years. If you expect that a particular asset will provide you an income of $30,000 in 12 years from now, that income stream would be worth $15,000 today, if inflation was 6% for the period. We have now discounted the cash flow of $30,000: It is only worth $15,000 for you at this moment.

Earnings before Interest

Earnings Before Interest and Tax includes all profits, operating and non-operating, before interest and income taxes are deducted. Earnings Before Interest and Tax (EBIT) is a traditional measurement method that does not include the cost of capital. Other words for EBIT are Operating Profit and Operating Earnings. The formula of EBIT is straightforward:

Net Sales
- *Operating Expenses*

Operating Profit (EBIT)

Earnings before interest, taxes, depreciation, and amortization, or EBITDA, came into wide use among private capital firms, wanting to calculate what they should pay for a business.

Here is the formula for calculating EBITDA:

```
  Net Sales
- Operating Expenses
-------------------------------------------------
  Operating Profit (EBIT)
+ Depreciation Expenses
+ Amortization Expenses
-------------------------------------------------
  EBITDA
```

Explanation of CAGR

Compound Annual Growth Rate is the average annual growth rate of an investment over a specified period of time. CAGR is calculated by taking the Nth root of the total percentage growth rate where N is the Number of Years in the period being considered.

$$CAGR = ((End\ Value\ /\ Begin\ Value)^{(1/N)}) - 1$$

CAGR can be used for the following applications:

1. Calculating and communicating the average returns of investment funds.
2. Demonstrating and comparing the performance of investment advisors.
3. Comparing the historical returns of stocks with Bonds or with a savings account.

Because CAGR assumes that an investment grows at a steady pace, CAGR is an imaginary conception because growth is never a steady function. It describes the growth of an investment as though it had grown at a steady pace.

Explanation of Current Ratio

The Current Ratio (CUR) measures the liquidity of a company by dividing all current assets by all current liabilities. It indicates a company's ability to pay short-term obligations. This ratio is also known as the working capital ratio and real ratio and is the standard measurement of a business' financial health. It will tell us whether a company is able to pay its current obligations by measuring if it has enough assets to cover its liabilities.

For example, if a corporation has M$50 in current assets to cover M$50 in current liabilities, this means that it has a Current Ratio of 1. Generally speaking, the more liquid the current assets, the smaller the CUR can be without cause for concern. For most industrial companies, 1.5 is an acceptable CUR. A standard CUR for a healthy business is close to two. This means the company has twice as many assets as liabilities.

Measuring Solvency

The Debt to Equity Ratio is used for Measuring Solvency and researching the Capital Structure of a company. It indicates how much the company is leveraged (in debt) by comparing what is owed to what is owned. In other words it measures a company's ability to borrow and repay money.

The Debt to Equity Ratio is closely watched by creditors and investors because it reveals the extent a company is willing to fund its operations with debt, rather than using equity. Lenders such as banks are particularly sensitive about this ratio, since an excessively high ratio of debt to equity will put their loans at risk of not being repaid. Banks can take action to counteract this problem by implementing restrictive contracts that force excess cash flow to repay debt. Restrictions on alternative use of cash are also quite common, as well as a requirement for investors to put more equity into the company themselves.

The Debt to Equity Ratio formula is fairly simple:

Divide Total Debt (= Total Liabilities) by Total Equity. Then multiply by 100 to get a percentage.
(Note that the Debt figure should include all operating and capital lease payments).

Balanced Scorecard

Recent management philosophy has shown the importance of customer focus and customer satisfaction. These are called leading indicators. If customers are not satisfied, they will find other suppliers that will meet their needs. Poor performance from this perspective is thus a leading indicator of future decline. See figure 8.1 on the following page.

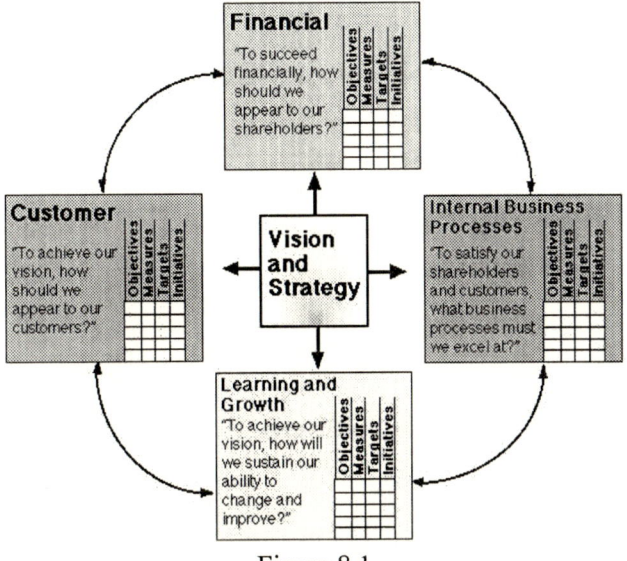

Figure 8.1

The 4 Perspectives of the Balanced Scorecard

The Balanced Scorecard is a strategic approach and performance management system that enables organizations to translate a company's vision and strategy into implementation, working from 4 perspectives:

1. *Financial perspective.*
2. *Customer perspective.*
3. *Business process perspective.*
4. *Learning and growth perspective.*

This allows the monitoring of present performance, but the method also tries to capture information about how well the organization is positioned to perform in the future.

The Balanced Scorecard provides the following benefits:

1. Focusing the whole organization on the few key things needed to create breakthrough performance.
2. Helps to integrate various corporate programs. Such as: quality, re-engineering, and customer service initiatives.
3. Breaking down strategic measures towards lower levels, so that unit managers, operators, and employees can see what's required at their level to achieve excellent overall performance.

Break-Even Point

The Break-even Point defines the point at which the gains equal the losses, when an investment will generate a positive return, the point where sales or revenues equal expenses. It also portrays total costs equaling total revenues. There is no profit made or loss incur red at the break-even point. This is important for anyone that manages a business, since the break-even point is the lower limit of profit when prices are set and margins are determined.

The Break-even method can be applied to a product, an investment, or the entire company's operations. Calculation of the BEP can be done using the following formula:

$$BEP = TFC / (SUP - VCUP)$$

where:

- BEP = break-even point (units of production)
- TFC = total fixed costs,
- VCUP = variable costs per unit of production,
- SUP = savings or additional returns per unit of production.

The main advantage of break-even analysis explains the relationship between cost, production volume and returns. It can be extended to show how changes in fixed cost-variable cost relationships, in commodity prices, or in revenues, will affect profit levels and break-even points. Break-even analysis is most useful when used with partial budgeting or capital budgeting techniques. The major benefit to using break-even analysis is that it indicates the lowest amount of business activity necessary to prevent losses.

Capital Asset

The Capital Asset Pricing Model (CAPM) estimates the value of stocks, securities, derivatives and/or assets by relating risk and expected return. CAPM is based on the idea that investors demand additional expected return (called the risk premium) if they are asked to accept additional risk.

The CAPM model says that the expected return that the investors will demand is equal to the rate on a risk-free security plus a risk premium. If the expected return is not equal to or higher than the required return, the investors will refuse to invest and the investment should not be undertaken.

According to CAPM, the marketplace compensates investors for taking systematic risk but not for taking specific risk. This is because specific risk can be diversified away. When an investor holds the market portfolio, each individual asset in that portfolio entails specific risk. But through diversification, the investor's net exposure is just the systematic risk of the market portfolio. The CAPM formula is:

Expected Security Return = Riskless Return + Beta x (Expected Market Risk Premium)
or: $r = Rf + Beta \times (RM - Rf)$

Cash Value Added

The Cash Value Added (CVA) model includes only an organization's cash items, i.e. Earnings Before Depreciation Interest and Tax (EBDIT, adjusted for non-cash charges), working capital movement and non-strategic investments. The sum of those three items is the Operating Cash Flow (OCF). The OCF is compared with a cash flow requirement, "the Operating Cash Flow Demand "(OCFD). This OCFD represents the cash flow needed to meet the investor's financial requirements on the company's strategic investments, i.e. the Cost of Capital.

Instead of measuring the investor's opportunity Cost of Capital in percentage terms, the CVA model uses the investor's opportunity Cost of Capital in cash terms. The difference between the OCF and the OCFD is the "Cash Value Added" - CVA. The CVA for a period is a good estimate of the cash flow generated above or below the investor's requirement for that period. This analysis can be done at each level of the company.

Unlike Securities measurements and Market-based measurements, CVA is a flow and can be used for performance evaluation over time.

Beyond Budgeting

Beyond Budgeting takes the first step in a long running battle to change organizations from centralized hierarchies towards devolved networks.

Firms have invested huge sums in quality programs, IT networks, process reengineering, and a range of management tools including EVA, balanced scorecards, and activity accounting. But they are unable to realize the new ideas because the budget and the command and control culture it supports remains predominant.

Beyond Budgeting (BB) is an alternative that is more adaptive and devolved. It replaces the budgeting model with a more adaptive and devolved alternative.

Experience Curve Effect

First described by Bruce Henderson in 1960, the Experience Curve Effect states that if a task is performed more often, the cost of performing the task will decrease. Researchers since then have observed experience curve effects for various industries ranging between 10 to 30 percent.

If a company can gain a big market share quickly in a new market, it has a competitive cost advantage because it can produce products cheaper than its competitors. Provided the cost savings are passed on to the buyers as price decreases, the company can sustain its advantage. If a company can accelerate its production experience by increasing its market share, it then can gain a cost advantage in its industry that would be hard to equal. The result is many companies try to gain a large market share quickly by investing heavily and aggressively pricing their products or services in new markets. Rapid growth must be kept in proportion to revenues generated, and the company must be careful about incurring debt in expansion. The debt may be a valuable investment and can be recovered later, once the company has become a market leader.

Fair Value Accounting

Originally defined by the Securities and Exchange Commission, Fair Value Accounting has two components. Fair Value of an asset is the amount at which that asset could be bought or sold in a current transaction between willing parties, other than in liquidation. On the other side of the balance sheet, the Fair Value of a liability is the amount at which that liability could be incurred or settled in a current transaction between willing parties, other than in liquidation.

If available, a quoted market price in an active market is the best evidence of Fair Value and should be used as the basis for the measurement. If a quoted market price is not available, preparers should make an estimate of Fair Value using the best information available in the circumstances. In many circumstances, quoted market prices are unavailable. As a result, making estimates of Fair Value is often difficult.

Today's markets are dynamic and volatile. Whether it is for buying or selling, what people want to know is what an asset is worth today. Fair Value accounting provides more transparency than historical cost based measurements.

Portfolio Analysis

A business portfolio is the collection of Strategic

Business Units that together form a corporation. The optimal business portfolio is one that fits perfectly to the company's strengths and helps to exploit the most attractive industries or markets.

A Strategic Business Unit (SBU) can either be an entire medium size company or a division of a large corporation. As long as it formulates its own business level strategy and has separate objectives from the parent company. Portfolio Analysis has three specific aims:

1. Analyze its current business portfolio and decide which SBU's should receive more or less investment

2. Develop growth strategies for adding new products and businesses to the portfolio

3. Decide which businesses or products should n o longer be retained

Systems Thinking

Systems Thinking analyzes complex feedback systems, such as the ones found in corporations and other social systems. In fact, it has been used to describe practically every sort of feedback system. System Dynamics is more or less the same as Systems Thinking, but emphasizes the usage of computer- simulation tools.

The term system means an interdependent group of things forming a unified pattern. Feedback refers to the situation of X affecting Y, and Y in turn affecting X, perhaps through a chain of causes and effects. One cannot study the link between

X and Y, and independently, the link between Y and X and predict how the system will behave. Only the study of the whole feedback system will lead to correct results. Here are the steps in the system Dynamics methodology:

1. Identify a problem,
2. Develop a dynamic hypothesis explaining the cause of the problem,
3. Build a computer simulation model of the system at the root of the problem,
4. Test the model to be certain that it reproduces the behavior seen in the real world,
5. Devise and test in the model alternative policies that alleviate the problem,
6. Implement the solution.

Absorption Costing Method or Full Costing

This is an inventory valuation model that includes all manufacturing costs. The Absorption Costing method includes direct materials direct labor, and both variable and fixed manufacturing overhead in the cost of a unit of product. As a result, under absorption costing, fixed overhead is a product cost until the products are sold.

Direct materials include those materials that become an integral part of a finished product, and which can be easily traced back into the finished product. Direct labor includes those factory labor costs that can be easily traced back to individual units of production.

Advocates of Absorption Costing say that it should

be included as part of inventories because of the production costs that are needed to create the products. Thus, they have "future economic benefits."

Advocates of Variable Costing argue that for a fixed manufacturing-cost to be an asset, it has to meet a "future cost avoidance" criteria. In the case of fixed manufacturing costs, they do not meet these criteria because they are incurred each time the production line opens. Thus, they should be regarded as expenses in that period, and only the variances in expenses should be inventoried.

Problems with absorption costing also include potential manipulations by plant managers, such as increasing production regardless of sales levels. In this way costs can be deferred to the next year, and a higher current profit can be shown for the sake of bonuses and promotions.

Capital Employed ROCE

ROCE is a ratio that indicates the efficiency and profitability of the capital investments of a company. In other words: the ROCE ratio is an indicator of how well a company is utilizing capital to generate revenue. ROCE should normally be higher than the borrowing rate from the company; otherwise any increase in borrowings will reduce shareholders' earnings.

The calculation of Return on Capital Employed is done by taking profit before interest and tax and dividing that by the difference between total assets and current liabilities.

Inclusive Value Measurement

The Inclusive Value Measurement Methodology is a rule-based mathematical model of multidimensional human - valuation that can be keyed into a wide range of applications in business, public sector, and engineering. This allows Inclusive Value Measurement to provide a way to manage and integrate diverse sources of value. See Figure 8.2 below.

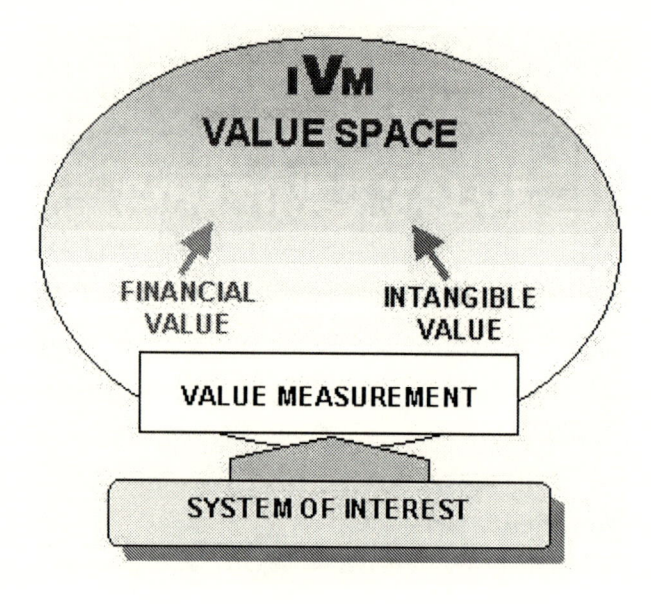

Figure 8.2

Value Measurement can be used to:

1. *Optimize Value for Money for businesses, services and projects.*
2. *Manage Cost-Benefit Analysis and life-cycle cost-effectiveness design projects.*
3. *Account properly for intangible value, such as: intellectual capital, reputation and information.*
4. *Establish the monetary equivalent of value contributions from intangible assets.*
5. *Provide a modeling environment for strategic*

decision-making and managing complexity.

6. *Conduct and visualize complex trade-offs between costs and benefits.*
7. *Serve as a valid measuring instrument for business value.*

Internal Rate of Return

The Internal Rate of Return (IRR) is the discount rate that delivers a net present value of zero for a series of future cash flows. It is a Discount Cash Flow (DCF) approach to valuation and investing. As with Net Present Value (NPV), IRR and NPV are widely used to decide which investments should be undertaken and which investments should be avoided.

The major difference between IRR and NPV is that while Net Present Value is expressed in monetary units (Euro's or Dollars for example), the IRR is the true interest yield expected from an investment expressed as a percentage.

Internal Rate of Return is the flip side of Net Present Value and is based on the same principles and the same calculations. PV shows the value of a stream of future cash flows discounted back to the present by some percentage that represents the minimum desired rate of return, often your company's cost of capital. IRR, on the other hand, computes a break-even rate of return. It shows the discount rate below which an investment causes a positive NPV (and should be made). And above which an investment causes a negative NPV (and should be avoided). It's the break-even discount rate, the rate at which the value of cash outflows equals the value of cash inflows.

The aim of the value-oriented manager should be to

invest in any project that has a positive NPV.

Human Capital

The Human Capital Index (HCI) of Watson Wyatt calculates the correlation of human capital and shareholder value. Watson Wyatt developed a set of measures quantifying exactly which Human Resources practices and policies have the greatest correlation to shareholder value.

Using those to assign a single Human Capital Index (HCI) "score" to each surveyed company allows them to deliver conclusive results. Where there are superior Human Resources practices, there is higher shareholder value. In other words: the Human Capital Index shows that if an organization is doing better in managing its human capital, it will also be better in its returns for shareholders. See Figure 8.3 below.

Figure 8.3

Intangible Assets

The Intangible Assets Monitor is interested in indicators that show a change and identify flows of knowledge. Ultimately the monitor should reveal how the intangible assets are developing and the growth of the asset in question, its renewal pace, how efficiently we are at utilizing it, and the risk that it ceases to exist.

The monitor can be used to design a management information system or to perform an audit. Only a few of the suggested indicators should be selected. The most important areas to cover are growth/renewal, efficiency and stability. The purpose is to get a broad picture, so one or two indicators in each category should be emphasized. See Figure 8.4 below.

Intangible Assets Monitor

	Market Value				
	Tangible Assets	Intangible Assets			
		External Structure	Internal Structure	Competence
Growth				
Innovation				
Efficiency				
Stability				

Figure 8.4

International Accounting Standards

International Accounting Standards decree authoritative guides pertaining to certain types of transaction and other events that are reflected in financial statements. Accordingly, compliance with accounting standards will normally be necessary for the fair presentation of financial statements that occur between nations.

Although the International Accounting Standards Committee has no formal authority to require compliance with its accounting standards, many countries and the European Commission require the financial statements of publicly-traded companies to be prepared in accordance with International Accounting Standards. However, Canada, Hong Kong, Japan, and the United States prohibit companies from using International Accounting Standards without complying with domestic accounting principles.

Mergers and Acquisitions

In Mergers and Acquisitions, the motto often traditionally was: "Make them like us". Or relatively simple criteria were used to choose an approach. The preferred Acquisition Integration Approaches are:

1. *Absorption. Management should be courageous to ensure that this vision for the acquisition is carried out.*
2. *Preservation. Management focus is: to keep the source of the acquired benefits intact, "nurturing".*
3. *Symbiosis. Management must ensure simultaneous boundary preservation and boundary permeability, gradual process.*
4. *Holding. No intention of integrating and value is created only by financial transfers, risk - sharing or general management capability.*

Also, a company should understand two (additional) criteria:

1. *The need for strategic interdependence.*
2. *The need for organizational autonomy.*

Managers must not lose sight of the fact that the strategic task of an acquisition is to create value. Furthermore they must not grant autonomy too quickly.

Value Profit Chain

The Value Profit Chain model was developed by James Heskett, Earl Sasser and Leonard Schlesinger. It argues that organizations need to focus on providing what their employees, customers, investors, suppliers, and others value most. Focusing on value will bring about necessary organizational change, and tying an organization to the most valued needs of it s customers will make it more responsive to its markets. In addition, giving employees what they appreciate in an organization will make them more productive and decrease the costs of employee turnover. The model predicts greater organizational effectiveness and profitability. The Value Profit Chain model acknowledges the importance of a company's three key constituents:

1. *Customers or clients,*
2. *Employees, and*
3. *Investors.*

The framework stresses the importance of the interrelationship of these three groups. Their behaviors can each be broken down into three areas:

1. Retention,
2. Related sales, and
3. Referrals.

Performance Risk and Valuation

The PRVit system is a proprietary performance, risk, and valuation method from Stern Stewart that relies on a purely quantitative stock rating and investment screening system. PRVit is derived from a cross-sectional and time series statistical analysis of the financial results of all Russell 3000 companies that is updated monthly. It compares a company with its sector peers and with the market universe in terms of its operating performance, risk, and key valuation multiples.

It compares the performance, risk and valuation compromises of each company with the market universe of such compromises to position a company on a relative valuation scale. The resulting overall PRVit -score - which runs from 0 to 100 - indicates the company's relative attractiveness as compared to the Russell 3000. A PRVit score of 50 thus indicates a fair balance among all three factors, and a seeming parity between the firm's intrinsic value and its traded value, given current market conditions. A high score however - in the range of 67 to 100 - indicates that an investor can acquire a considerable amount of valuable performance potential for a reasonable valuation price, and thus the stock may have stored up the potential to outperform the market if past trends are sustained. A low score, say from 0 to 33, indicates that the company's market deemed likely to perform less than the overall market.

Real Options

Real Options capture the value of managerial flexibility to adapt strategic decisions in response to unexpected market developments. A company creates shareholder value by identifying Real Options, managing of Real Options, and exercising Real Options, associated with its investment portfolio. The Real Options method applies financial options theory to quantify the value of management flexibility, thus turning uncertainty to its advantage in a changing world.

When valuations involve significant future flexibility or uncertainty and/or future cash-flows alone are close to break-even, flexibility is a major source of value, and option value must be taken into consideration. Generally, the following variables determine the value of having (an) option(s) - option value:

1. *Time to expiration (duration).*
2. *Degree of uncertainty.*
3. *Cost of acquiring the option(s).*
4. *Potential cash flows lost, compared to full upfront commitment.*
5. *Risk-free interest rate.*
6. *Expected present value of future cash flows.*

By introducing these factors into business decision-making, the Real Options method has enabled corporate decision-makers to use uncertainty for the advantage of the firm and to create a limit to downside risk.

Return on Invested Capital

ROIC measures the historical performance of a business unit or of an entire company. High (relative) ROIC levels are seen as proof of a strong company and/or solid company management. However, a high ROIC may just as well be an indicator of poor management, caused by harvest behavior, by ignoring growth possibilities, and by long –term value destruction.

Here is how ROIC is calculated:

$$ROIC = \frac{\text{Net Income After Tax}}{\text{Invested Capital}} = \frac{\text{After Tax Operating Earnings}}{\text{Total Assets - Excess Cash - Non-Interest-Bearing Current Liabilities}}$$

More accurately, ROIC for a single time period = Net Operating Earnings before Interest and Amortization Charges, but after Cash Taxes

Total Assets - Excess Cash - Non-Interest-Bearing Current Liabilities

Since Return on Invested Capital is an accounting-based measure, it suffers the following potential concerns:

1. *Can be manipulated by management,*
2. *Is influenced by accounting conventions and by changes in accounting conventions, and*
3. *Is affected by inflation and currency exchange movements.*

Risk Adjusted Return on Capital

RAROC uses a risk-adjusted framework to measure and manage profitability. The tool reads risk-adjusted financial performance and provides a uniform view of profitability across businesses (Strategic Business Units / divisions). RAROC and related concepts such as RORAC and RARORAC are mainly used within (business lines of) banks and insurance companies. RAROC is defined as the ratio of risk-adjusted return to economic capital.

RAROC systems allocate capital for two basic reasons: (1) risk management and (2) performance evaluation. For risk-management purposes, the main goal of allocating capital to individual business units is to determine the bank's optimal capital structure. This process involves estimating how much the risk (volatility) of each business unit contributes to the total risk of the bank and, hence, to the bank's overall capital requirements.

For performance-evaluation purposes, RAROC systems assign capital to business units. As part of a process of determining the risk-adjusted rate of return and, ultimately, the economic value added of each business unit. The economic value added of each business unit, defined in detail below, is simply the unit's adjusted net income less a capital charge (the amount of equity capital allocated to the unit times the required return on equity). The objective in this case is to measure a business unit's contribution to shareholder value for effective Capital budgeting and incentive compensation at the Business Unit level.

Shareholder Value Perspective

The Shareholder Value Perspective emphasizes

profitability over responsibility and sees organizations primarily as instruments of its owners. Shareholder Value proponents believe that the success of an organization can be measured by such indicators as share price, dividends and economic profit. They regard Stakeholder Management rather as a means than as an end/purpose in itself. They believe that social responsibility is not a matter for organizations, and think that society is best served by organizations pursuing self-interest and economic efficiency.

The Shareholder Value philosophy is not blind for the demands placed on corporations by other stakeholders than the shareholders. The purpose of a company is first and foremost to maximize shareholder value. Advocates of the Shareholder Value Perspective are convinced that society is best served by economic rationale. Responsibility for employment, local communities, the environment, consumer welfare, and social developments are not organizational matters, but should be dealt with by individuals and governments. By pursuing enlightened self-interest and by maintaining market-based relations between the corporation and all stakeholders, the pursuing of maximum value for the shareholders will also result in maxi-mizing society's wealth.

Parenting Advantage

The Parenting Advantage model describes how a parent company can create value. In their article, "From Corporate Strategy to Parenting Advantage", Michael Goold and Andrew Campbell argue that the parent company should not only add value to a business unit, but add more value than any other potential parent - they call this: "Parenting Advantage".

In their book: "Corporate -Level Strategy: Creating Value in the Multi - business Company", they mention four types of parental value creation:

1. *Stand-alone influence. Each subsidiary is viewed as a separate profit center. Using basic performance targets, the businesses are controlled and monitored. Value creation is provided by making strategic decisions such as the appointment of managers and approving major capital expenditures.*
2. *Linkage influence. Value is created by improved co-operation and synergy benefits.*
3. *Central functions and services. Corporate value is created through the provision of administrative and managerial services to the businesses.*
4. *Corporate development. Value creation through portfolio management.*

The corporate center should not be just another layer of accounting, but must add value by enunciating the strategic architecture and manage the financial resources among the business units.

Relative Value of Growth

The Relative Value of Growth framework (RVG) from Nathaniel J. Mass can be used for comparing the way growth - and margin improvement effect shareholder value. The relative value of growth expresses the value of an extra percentage point of growth as a multiple of the value of a percentage point increase in a company's operating profit margin. If the multiple is higher, the growth will be more valuable to a company.

An RVG of 3, for example, means that a firm would generate three times as much shareholder value by adding 1% of growth, than it would add by increasing operating profit by 1%. The relative Value of Growth model has a number of uses:

1. Making investing decisions.
2. Corporate Strategy formulation.
3. Business Strategy formulation.
4. Establishing a long -term focus.
5. Show the potential of growth as a source of value.
6. Understanding shareholders expectations.
7. Performance Management.

Strategic Stakeholder Management

In this formulation, stakeholder management is part of a company's strategy but in no way drives that strategy. Implicit in this perspective is the assumption that unproductive modes will be discontinued, as will those that involve resources that are no longer needed. The concerns of stakeholders only enter a firm's decision-making processes if they have strategic value for the firm.

Two variants of the Strategic Stakeholder Management approach are the direct effects model and the moderation model. In the direct effects model, the attitudes and the actions of managers toward stakeholders (their stakeholder orientation) are perceived as having a direct effect on firm financial performance, independent of the corporate strategy. In the moderation model, the managerial orientation toward stakeholders does impact the corporate strategy by moderating the relationship between strategy and financial performance.

The following 12 principles of the Network Economy were designed to provide new rules for the Internet era:

1. *The Law of Connection. Embrace the unlimited possibilities the Internet provides.*
2. *The Law of Plentitude. More gives more: Mathematicians have proven that the sum of a network increases as the square of the number of members.*
3. *The Law of Exponential Value. Success is nonlinear: During its first 10 years, Microsoft's profits were negligible. Its profits rose above the background noise only around 1985. But once they began to rise, they exploded.*
4. *The Law of Tipping Points. Significance precedes momentum. In biology, the tipping points of fatal diseases are fairly high, but in technology, they seem to trigger at much lower percentages.*
5. *The Law of Increasing Returns. Make virtuous circles: Value explodes with membership, and the value explosion sucks in more members.*
6. *The Law of Inverse Pricing. The price and quality curves diverge so dramatically with technology that it sometimes seems as if*

the better something is, the cheaper it will be.

7. *The Law of Generosity. Since compounding network knowledge inverts prices, the marginal cost of an additional copy drops to near zero. Flooding the market with a product can make it indispensable. Once a product has become indispensable, the company sells auxiliary services or upgrades, enabling it to continue its generosity and maintaining this marvelous circle.*

8. *The Law of the Allegiance. When networks develop indistinguishable characteristics, the vital difference between any two networks becomes less meaningful in a Network Economy.*

9. *The Law of Devolution. In the Network Economy, the ability to relinquish a product or occupation or industry at its peak will be priceless.*

10. *The Law of Displacement. No longer will anyone ask the question "How big will online commerce be?" because all commerce is jumping onto the Internet.*

11. *The Law of "Churn". Seek sustainable disequilibrium: "Churn" topples the incumbent and creates a platform that is ideal for more innovation and birth.*

12. *The Law of Inefficiencies. Don't solve*

problems, seek opportunities. In the Network Economy, our ability to solve our social and economic problems will be limited primarily by our lack of imagination in seizing opportunities.

PE or PEG Ratio

The P/E ratio is a common measure of relative value of equities based on their earnings per share. Equities with high P/E ratios suggest a market consensus that the firm has strong future earnings growth prospects. Because the P/E ratio does not reflect future earnings growth, the PEG ratio is used to determine whether the market valuation is supported by the predicted future earnings growth rates.

PEG ratio = (Market Price / Earnings Per Share) / (Predicted Annual Growth in Earnings)

Portfolio managers and analysts commonly compare PEG ratios to identify undervalued and overvalued equities. A common application is applied to emerging market equities (where earnings growth rates are high and uncertain). As a general rule of thumb, when the PEG ratio is approaching a value of 1.0, the firm's equity is considered "fairly" valued. If the PEG ratio is less than 1.0, the equities are considered "undervalued". If the PEG ratio is greater than 1.0, the equities are considered "overvalued".

Since the market tends to price equities relative to their sector, a meaningful comparison of PEG ratios (an d P/E ratios) demands viewing them against the sector or industry average.

Performance Prism

The Performance Prism has advantages over other frameworks because it covers all stakeholders of an organization, investors, customers & intermediaries, employees, suppliers, regulators and communities. It does this in two ways: by considering what the wants and the needs are of the stakeholders, and, uniquely, what the organization wants and needs from its stakeholders. In this way, the reciprocal relationship with each stakeholder is examined.

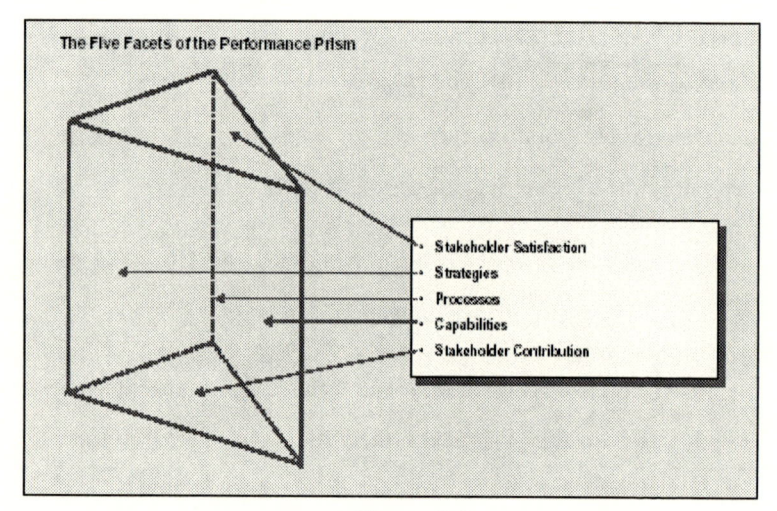

Figure 8.5

The Performance Prism consists of five facets:

1. *Stakeholder Satisfaction.*
2. *Stakeholder Contribution.*
3. *Strategies.*
4. *Processes.*
5. *Capabilities.*

The Performance Prism illustrates the hidden complexity

of our corporate world. One dimensional, traditional frameworks pick up elements of this complexity. While each framework offers a unique perspective on performance, it is essential to recognize that this is all that they offer: a single uni - dimensional perspective on performance. Performance, however, is not uni - dimensional. To understand it in its entirety, it is essential to view from the multiple and interlinked perspectives offered by the Performance Prism.

Product Life Cycle

The Product Life Cycle concept has significant impact upon business strategy and corporate performance. The Product Life Cycle method identifies the distinct stages affecting sales of a product, from the product's inception until its retirement.

Any company is constantly seeking ways to grow future cash flows by maximizing revenue from the sale of products and services. Cash Flow allows a company to maintain its viability, invest in new product development and improve its workforce. This effort helps acquire additional market share and make the company a leader in its respective industry.

Although the product life cycle for many modern products is shrinking, the operating life of many products is lengthening. For example, the operating life of some durable goods, such as automobiles and appliances, has increased substantially. As a result, the companies that produce these products must take their market life and service life into account when they are planning. Increasingly, companies are attempting to optimize revenue and profits over the entire life cycle.

Profit Pools

The Profit Pools model states that managers or companies must focus on profits, rather than on revenue growth. The theory calls for managers to look beyond revenues to see the shape of their industry's profit pool. In this way strategies can be created which result in profitable growth. The Profit Pool model can be used to:

1. Identify new sources of profit.
2. Rethink the role of a company in the Value Chain.
3. Refocusing a company on its traditional sources of profit.
4. Make product decisions, pricing decisions and operational decisions

Although the concept is simple, the structure of Profit Pools is usually quite complex. The pool will be deeper in some segments of the value chain than in others, and depths will vary within an individual segment as well. For example, the profitability of a segment may vary widely by customer group, product category, geographic market, and distribution channel. Moreover, the pattern of profit concentration in an industry will often differ from the pattern of revenue concentration.

Quick Ratio

The Quick Ratio method measures the liquidity of a company. It converts all assets into cash and divides the result by all current liabilities. It specifically excludes inventory. It is an indicator of the extent to which a company can pay current liabilities without having to rely on the sale of inventory. Typically, a Quick Ratio of 1:1 or higher is good, and indicates a company does not have to rely on the sale of inventory to pay the bills.

Market Value Added

Market Value Added (MVA) is the difference between the equity market valuation of a listed/quoted company and the sum of the adjusted book value of debt and equity invested in the company. It calculates the sum of all capital claims held against the company, the market value of debt and the market value of equity. Here is the Market Value Added formula:

Market Value Added (MVA) = Market Value - Invested Capital

A high MVA indicates the company has created substantial wealth for the shareholders. MVA is equivalent to the present value of all future expected Economic Value Added. Negative MVA means that the value of the actions and investments of management is less than the value of the capital contributed to the company by the capital markets. This means that wealth or value has been destroyed.

The aim of a firm should be to maximize MVA. The aim should not be to maximize the value of the firm, since this can be easily accomplished by investing ever-increasing amounts of capital.

Net Present Value

The Net Present Value (NPV) of an investment (project) is the difference between the sum of the discounted cash flows that are expected from the investment, and the amount that is initially invested. This traditional valuation method (often for a project) works in harmony with the Discounted Cash Flow measurement methodology, whereby the following steps are undertaken:

The following three steps are used to calculate the Net Present Value:

> 1. Calculation of expected free cash flows (often per year) that result out of the investment
> 2. Subtract / discount for the cost of capital (an interest rate to adjust for time and risk)
> *The intermediate result is called: Present Value.*
> 3. Subtract the initial investments

> Note: The end result is called: Net Present Value.

Therefore, NPV is an amount that expresses how much value an investment will generate. This is done by measuring all cash flows over time back towards the current point in present time. If the NPV method results in a positive amount, the project should be undertaken.

NOPAT

NOPAT is the Operating Profit minus taxes. Another word for Net Operating Profit After Tax is Profit after Tax. Here is how it is calculated:

Net Sales

- *Operating Expenses*

Operating Profit

- *Taxes*

NET OPERATING PROFIT AFTER TAX (NOPAT)

NOPAT is necessary for calculating economic value added. NOPAT can be calculated at divisional (Strategic Business Unit) level. Net Operating Profit After Tax (NOPAT) does NOT, however, take into account the idea that a business must cover both the operating costs AND the capital costs.

Operating Profit Percentage

The Operating Profit Percentage reveals the return from standard operations, excluding the impact of extraordinary items and other comprehensive income. It shows the extent to which a company is earning a profit from standard operations. As opposed to resorting to asset sales or unique transactions to post an 'artificial' profit.

Calculation of the Operating Profit Percentage is straightforward: subtract the costs of goods sold, as well as all sales, general, and administrative expenses, from sales. Divide the result by sales. To obtain a percentage that is related strictly to operational results, be sure to exclude interest income and expense from the calculation, since these items are related to a company's financing decisions rather than its operational characteristics. Expense totals used in the Operating Profit

Percentage ratio should exclude extraordinary transactions, as well as asset dispositions, since they do not relate to continuing operations.

Payback Period

The Payback Period method focuses on recovering the cost of investments. The Payback Period represents the amount of time that it takes for a capital budgeting project to recover its initial cost. Calculating the Payback Period can be done in the following way:

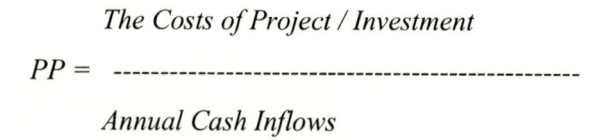

$$PP = \frac{\textit{The Costs of Project / Investment}}{\textit{Annual Cash Inflows}}$$

The Payback Period concept holds that all other things being equal, the better investment is the one with the shorter payback period. For example, take a project costing a total of $200,000. The expected returns of the project amount to $40,000 annually. The Payback Period would be $200,000 : $40,000 = 5 years.

Value Based Management

Value Based Management (VBM) can be defined in two ways. The first is to ensure that corporations are managed consistently to produce maximum shareholder value. The second definition of Value Based Management aims to provide consistency of:

1. the corporate mission (business philosophy),
2. the corporate strategy to achieve the corporate

mission and purpose,
3. corporate governance (who determines the corporate mission and regulates the activities of the corporation),
4. the corporate culture,
5. corporate communication,
6. organization of the corporation,
7. decision processes and systems,
8. performance management processes and systems, and
9. reward processes and systems.

Value Based Management consists of three parts:

1. *Creating Value. How the company can increase or generate maximum future value. More or less equal to strategy.*
2. *Managing for Value. Governance, change management, organizational culture, communication, leadership.*
3. *Measuring Value. Valuation.*

Value Based Management is dependent on the corporate purpose and the corporate values. The corporate purpose can either be economic (Shareholder Value) or can also aim at other constituents directly (Stakeholder Value).

Value Reporting

Designed by Pricewaterhouse Coopers, the Value Reporting Framework measures and manages corporate performance and structuring communications. The traditional corporate reporting model no longer meets the needs of the companies that report on their performance to investors and other stakeholders. Value Reporting is PricewaterhouseCoopers' innovative approach for performance measurement and corporate reporting. It was designed to meet investors' needs for more and better information.

Value Reporting supplements traditional financial reporting by helping companies provide a more detailed, transparent picture of their performance regarding market opportunities, strategy, risks, intangible assets, and other important non-financial value drivers.

Market Overview	Strategy	Value Creating Activities	Financial Performance
• Competitive Environment • Regulatory Environment • Macro-economic Environment	• Goals and Objectives • Organisational Design • Governance	• Customers • People • Innovation • Brands • Supply Chain • Environmental, Social and Ethical	• Financial Position • Risk Profile • Economic Performance • Segmental Analysis • Accounting Policies

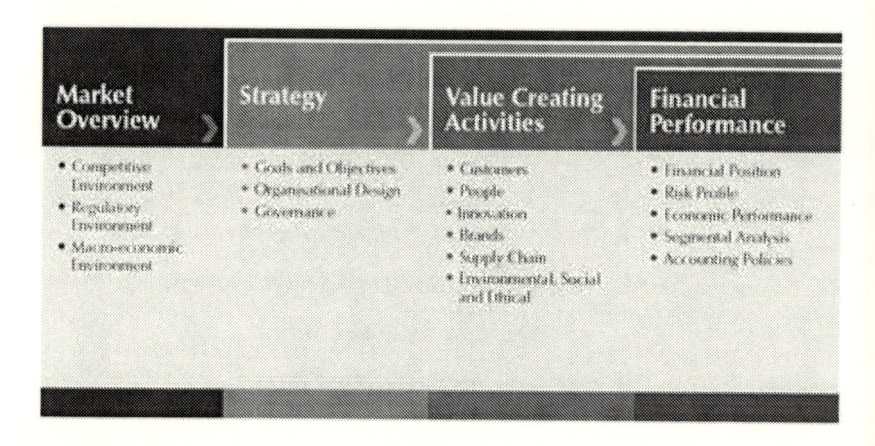

Figure 8.6

Based on PricewaterhouseCoopers' capital markets research, the Framework provides a structure for internal and external reporting of both financial and non-financial information along broad categories. Market Overview, Value Strategy, Managing for Value and Value Platform. Each is broken down into specific elements for more detailed

242

and transparent reporting. The Value Platform category, for example, includes all activities and relationships that underpin how the company creates value. These include such intangible and non-financial measures as products, customers, people, innovation, supply chain and corporate reputation.

WACC or Weighted Average Cost of Capital

Corporations create value for shareholders by earning a return on the invested capital that is above the cost of that capital. WACC (Weighted Average Cost of Capital) is an expression of this cost. It is used to see if value is added when certain intended investments or strategies or projects or purchases are undertaken.

WACC is expressed as a percentage, like interest. For example, if a company works with a WACC of 12%, than this means that only investments should be made and all investments should be made, that give a return higher than the WACC of 12%.

The costs of capital for any investment, whether for an entire company or for a project, is the rate of return which capital providers would want to receive if they invested their capital elsewhere. In other words, costs of capital are a type of opportunity cost.

Here is the WACC formula:

Debt / Total Financing (cost of debt)(1-Tax)
+ Equity / Total Financing (cost of equity)

WACC

Let's look at an example. Suppose the following situation in a company:

The market value of debt = €300 million
The market value of equity = €400 million
The cost of debt = 8%
The corporate tax rate = 35%
The cost of equity is 18%

The WACC of this company is:

300 : 700 * 8% * (1-35%)
+ 400 : 700 * 18%

12,5% (WACC - Weighted Average Cost of Capital)

Direct Costing, Variable Costing, Marginal Costing

The variable costing method creates an inventory valuation/costing model that includes only the variable manufacturing costs in the cost of a unit of product. It is also called direct costing or marginal costing. The Variable Manufacturing costs are:

1. Direct materials. Those materials that become an integral part of a finished product and can be conveniently traced into it.
2. Direct labor. Those factory labor costs that can be easily traced into individual

units of product. Also called: touch labor.
3. Only variable manufacturing overhead costs are included. The entire amounts of fixed costs are expenses in the year incurred.

Variable Costing is also referred to as the Direct Costing method or the Marginal Costing method.

Total Business Return

Total Business Return is a forward-looking measurement of Cash Flow Return on Investment. TBR was designed to imitate the way in which capital markets determine Total Shareholder Return (TSR). In this way we can also use Total Business Return for an internal business unit, division, project or strategy. Here is how the Total Business Return is calculated:

Terminal Value at the End of the Period
- *Gross Cash Investments at the Begin of the Period*
+ *Gross Cash Flows in the In-between Period*

Total Business Return (TBR)

Total Business Return is very similar to something EVA users call forward looking IRR. TBR can be calculated at divisional (Strategic Business Unit) level and below. Total Business Return can even be observed for privately held companies.

Total Cost of Ownership

The Total Cost of Ownership (TCO) method calculates all associated costs of an asset over a given time period. Some examples of assets are: a building, software or a truck. It can be described as the cost of owning and operating an asset over time. TCO does not only reflect the costs of purchase. It also includes all other aspects in the further use and maintenance of the asset.

There is no broad accepted formula for TCO. You need to consider all relevant costs that are related to an asset.

The following list contains typical cost elements of Total Cost of Ownership:

1. *Purchase price.*
2. *Installation cost.*
3. *Commissioning cost.*
4. *Energy costs. Repair costs.*
5. *Upgrade costs.*
6. *Conversion costs.*
7. *Training costs.*
8. *Support costs.*
9. *Service costs.*
10. *Maintenance costs.*
11. *Downtime costs.*
12. *Safety costs.*
13. *Productivity costs.*
14. *Risk cost.*
15. *Disposal costs.*
16. *Financing costs.*

Which factors should you use? This depends upon the industry where the asset will be used and the characteristics of the asset.

Total Shareholder Return

Total Shareholder Return (TSR) represents the change in capital value of a listed/quoted company over a period (typically 1 year or longer), plus dividends, expressed as a plus or minus percentage of the opening value.

Here is how the total Shareholder Return is calculated:

(Share Price at the end of the period - Share Price at the beginning of the period + Dividends) / Share Price at the beginning of the period = Total Shareholder Return.

It should be noted that dividends include not only regular dividend payments, but also include any cash payments to shareholders, and also include special or one-time dividends, and also include share buybacks.

TSR can be easily compared from company to company and benchmarked against industry or market returns without having to worry about a bias regarding size because Total Shareholder Return is a percentage.

Afterword

Today's organizations are in a constant state of flux. The 21st century business environment may be likened to an experiment in "Brownian motion". Increased competition and stakeholders' demand for more return on investment continues to create a sense of urgency for organizations to get it 'right' or be extinct. The recent corporate America's debacle has brought corporation under increased scrutiny and the terms "business ethics" and "corporate social responsibility" have since ascended new meanings. Consequently, there seem to be an endless quest for ways to improve the organization with the only constant being change itself. These are some of the reasons why Applied Change Management is such a relevant text, today and for the future.

In eight short chapters, Applied Change Management weaved a beautiful tapestry through the subject of change management and organizational transformation. Dr. McCollum began with an introduction to organizational development as a practical approach to change and transformation in organizations. Under such topics as: business ethics and corporate responsibility, communication and leadership, marketing and branding, human resources strategy, decision-making and valuation, program and project management, organizational change and transformation and finance and investment, Applied Change Management provided the reader with a rich pedigree of proven techniques and processes for sustainable change management.

Throughout the industrial age and to some degree the early part of what we commonly refer to as the "electronic age", corporations were thought to exist for the purpose of making profits. Over ninety percent of most company's annual report consists of a multitude of financial metrics such as EBIT, EBIAT, EPS and the list goes on. Although this has not changed much, there is however a heightened interest in the role of businesses and corporation as a conduit for positive social change. Never a time, it seems, have there been more clarion calls for corporations to consider the interest of stakeholders, employees, society and the environment above all others. For these reasons, I believe that Applied Change Management's treatment of business ethics and corporate responsibility as one of the corner stones for organizational transformation is indeed a higher level of thinking. With discussions of concepts such as the "Clarkson principles for stakeholder management", "soft systems methodology" and the "bottom of the pyramid" Dr. McCollum provided the reader the awareness and strong foundation to delve into more details in understanding ethical issues and social responsibility.

Dr. McCollum understands that leadership and communication are critical success factors for change management. The mediocre performance of corporate change and transformation initiatives such as business process reengineering (BPR), total quality management (TQM) and other contemporary management maxims can be inextricably linked to patterns of ineffective communication and poor leadership. In Applied Change Management, proven strategies for effective communications were offered to the reader. Dr. McCollum discussed consensus-seeking theory based on the work of Irving Janis. Scenarios have long been used as one of the premier forecasting technique, "scenarios are a discrete, internally consistent views of how the world will look in the future, which can be selected to bound the probable range of outcomes that might feasibly occur", writes Porter (1980). In Applied Change

Management, the concept of scenario planning was operationalized thereby making the concept easier for practitioners seeking to use it for planning or as a means of communication. Dr. McCollum introduced the reader to the leadership continuum from autocratic through to democratic leadership and espoused contemporary leadership theories such as the path-goal theory, contingency theory, level 5 leadership and expectancy theory.

The era of "build it and they will come" - an era when companies believed that the customer should be glad that they existed is far past. Today, customer needs drives company objectives, a culture that has facilitated the evolution of the company from the production era to the marketing era. This is no more evident than the fact that one would hardly find a corporation in America without a marketing department, some call it business development. In Applied Change Management, the importance of marketing and the influence of branding as yet another process for organizational change and transformation are accentuated. Dr. McCollum discussed Porter's competitive five force model while providing a synopsis of the book "competitive strategy".

In my opinion, human resources are the most important strategic asset of the corporation yet so many change initiatives are skewed in favor of processes, tools and technology. Applied Change Management elegantly put together a set of best practice approaches to "human resources strategy". Elucidating the works of Geert Hofstede, Edward Deming and Aldeerfer's amongst others, Dr. McCollum offered the interested reader a rich background of theories that are applicable to sustainable human resource management. Applied Change Management integrated theory and practice by presenting practical models and concepts such as; People Capability Maturity Model (PCMM), cultural intelligence, and emotional intelligence.

A vital aspect of successful change management initiatives is the change driver's ability to make the right choices amongst a myriad of plausible options. Therefore it is important to understand the multiplicity of available decision-making processes and tools that will enhance the quality of choice which will optimally impact the change initiative. Beginning with the basic decision making steps, Dr. McCollum described more scientific decision making methods including: probability and statistical inference, optimization, artificial intelligence, neural networks and more operational systems such as data mining and business analytics.

How many organizations today talk about teams, self directed work groups and the many forms of work clusters that has become synonymous with the contemporary organization? These groups pursue a common objective within a defined time frame, cost and quality constraints. Such common objectives or tasks are referred to as projects; a program on the other hand has so many similar characteristics of a project with the distinctive attributes of being ongoing and does not necessarily have to be unique. With the numerous publications on the subject of program and project management; Applied Change Management makes a significant contribution by briefly introducing the reader to some of the more important concepts of program and project management - from Earned Value Management (EVM) to managing projects and portfolio as a means to realizing the organization's strategic objectives. Applied Change Management introduced its readers to the "five evolutionary stages in managing organizational processes" based on the widely acclaimed capability maturity model – one of the many areas in which the author is a subject matter expert.

Organizational change and transformation a sub-title to the text and appropriately so, here the author presented a plethora of business model approaches and frameworks – In Applied Change Management, Dr. McCollum noted that "renowned business strategy gurus adhere to the business model based on the three C's" – corporation, competition and customer. Using theories proposed by seminal author such as Peter Senge – five disciplines, Wilfred Kruger – change management iceberg, Anita McGahan – trajectory of industry change, Harison Trice – changing organizational culture; Applied Change Management succinctly illustrate core transformational methodologies that organizations have utilized to impact social change.

Applied Change Management also highlighted many key finance and investments terms and measures. Understanding these fundamentals of corporate finance and investments is important to a corporation's leadership as well as its stakeholders.

In Applied Change Management, Dr. McCollum coherently put together for its audience a detailed yet easy to understand explanations of concepts often taught in a typical MBA class in finance. Relevant topics such as cash flows, ROE, Ratios and the prediction of bankruptcy were examined. In doing so Applied Change Management is valuable to readers interested in understanding the practices and techniques commonly used by finance professionals. Dr. McCollum offered insights on how to understand and interpret financial statements as one of the key sources of information for financial decision making. With lucidity, Dr. McCollum defined concepts such as, NPV, Payback rule, WACC, CAPM, and Valuation. These are relevant and solid information for the analyzing and identifying potential business project and investment decisions. Applied Change Management is definitely a light for a future path to finance and investment.

I expect Applied Change Management to be a very valuable instrument in the arsenal of the organizational development practitioner, the change agent and the scholar who seeks a one stop library of change management concepts. I believe that scholar-practitioners will embrace Applied Change management as a powerful tool for organizational change and transformation. In my opinion, Applied Change Management fills a void in the available literature on change management. The ideas presented are those of accomplished authorities in their field. It is an invaluable guide to great ideas, a recipe yet non-prescriptive lexicon of potent organizational transformation thoughts, processes and models. Asked to sum up Applied Change Management in four words I would say; 'complex ideas made simple'.

Charles Ebebiri, PhD Candidate
Walden University

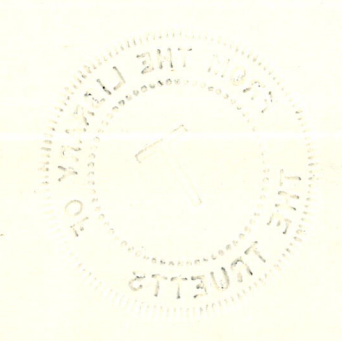

Printed in the United States
87868LV00002B/298/A